HOW TO LEAD AND MOTIVATE OTHERS

This book is dedicated to
my beloved husband Bob,
one of the finest human beings I know.

IRIS BARROW

HOW TO LEAD AND MOTIVATE OTHERS

key skills for effective leadership

CEDAR
New Zealand

By the same author

Fifteen Steps to Overcome Anxiety and Depression
From Strength to Strength
Know Your Strengths and Be Confident
Relax and Come Alive
You Can Communicate
You Can Do It!
Your Marriage Can Work

Published by Cedar New Zealand, an imprint of Reed Publishing (NZ) Ltd, 39 Rawene Road, Birkenhead, Auckland 10. Associated companies, branches and representatives throughout the world.

ISBN 0 7900 0475 5

First published by Reed Books 1995
Reprinted by Cedar New Zealand 1996

Printed by Brebner Print, New Zealand

CONTENTS

ACKNOWLEDGEMENTS

For mental stimulation and reference, my thanks to: Professor Hans Seyle, Dr John Sturt, Dr Steven Saunders, C.B.A. (Christian Broadcasting Association), K. Albrecht & Prentice Hall, Drs Friedman & Rosenham.

I would especially like to thank my husband Bob Barrow and my personal assistant Bernice Bormans, without whose input, effort and encouragement this book may not have been written.

I would also like to thank Nigel Armstrong of First Training for his encouragement and helpful comments on the manuscript.

I acknowledge the many people whose writings and sayings have influenced my work and from whom I have quoted, in particular:

Brown, H. Jackson Jnr. *P.S. I Love You.* Nashville, Tennessee, Rutledge Hill Press, 1991.

Harris, Thomas A. *I'm Okay – You're Okay.* London, Pan, 1973.

Hayward, Susan, and Cohan, Nigel, eds. *Bag of Jewels.* Avalon, In-tune Books, 1987.

Le Boeuf, Michael. *How to Motivate People.* Melbourne, Schwartz & Wilkinson Publishers, 1990.

Also Akio Morita, chairman of Sony, and Stephen Jobs, co-founder of Apple Computer Inc.

I have on occasion used extracts from my books *Your Marriage Can Work, You Can Do It!, From Strength to Strength* and *You Can Communicate,* published by Reed Books.

All names used in case histories are fictitious and do not relate to any living person.

CHAPTER ONE

Why people in the workforce lose motivation and enthusiasm

What makes a successful leader? As a human resources consultant to industry I have had the opportunity of working with people at all levels in the workforce. This has given me an insight which would have been difficult to gain in any other field of work. In presenting seminars and training sessions and also in counselling people I have, I believe, developed a feel for what makes a successful leader and a successful motivator — the two are almost inseparable, the one being ineffectual without the other.

I have observed certain essential qualities in the true leaders, certain strengths, characteristics and skills which they all exhibit. Many people have outstanding talents and skills which are invaluable in their particular field, but they are not necessarily leaders who know how to motivate people. Leadership qualities and motivational skills have to be learnt, and can be — if the person has the right attitude and the commitment necessary to do so. It is these qualities and skills we shall explore in this book.

As we proceed some qualities will be explored in greater depth and will therefore warrant a chapter of their own. However all of the strengths and skills I will describe are necessary if the leader is to motivate people to give of their best in the working situation. All lead to a higher level of self-motivation which, in turn, leads to better results. It is now becoming increasingly accepted in industry that an organisation's strengths lie not so much in its technology but in its people. If those people can be made to feel that they are important and valuable members of a team which is working to achieve clearly defined goals and objectives, their performance is more likely to be good, and in fact will often exceed expectations.

I know this to be so through having run a seminar and counselling agency over several years. Though a small business, we have had a number of staff (including counsellors) working for us throughout the time we have been operating. So in a sense I am speaking from the horse's mouth as well as from experience with business organisations both large and small. And what I have come to believe is the most demotivating factor of all is for people to feel that they are merely *tools in the workforce* and not *valuable and valued members of a highly motivated team* who are committed to achieving specified objectives and long-term goals. If they feel themselves to be the former, motivation will certainly decrease — as will efficiency, and then productivity.

PEOPLE ARE YOUR GREATEST RESOURCE

I have observed so many times the disastrous consequences which result when management fails to instil this feeling of worth and team loyalty in their personnel. Considerable emphasis may be put on obtaining the best equipment, technology and systems, all of which are important, but too often very little attention is given to what makes the organisation tick — its people. In running a successful business a high priority must be to have loyal, committed and satisfied people. If you have this you have everything, and usually all else begins to fall into place. Without it you are sailing into dangerous waters. It is such a simple principle, but one which is too often overlooked or neglected.

In any work situation people will either be feeling 'This organisation cares about me and the part I play in making it successful', or they will be feeling 'This organisation does not value me, but only aims to extract the most it can from me in work and service'. In the latter case the employee is automatically demotivated and will usually develop a defensive reaction, for instance, 'I'm going to look after number one and do what is necessary to hold my job.' 'I'm only working for money; this is the only reason I turn up to work each day.' Multiply these negative attitudes many times and what do you think the likely end consequence for any business will be? If this sounds extreme, believe me it is not. I am speaking from the experience of having observed people at all levels in business. As an impartial outsider brought in to give training sessions, or as a human resources trouble-shooter, I also find that people will speak freely to me. Admittedly I make the opportunity for them to do so, but I can best serve the organisation I am working for by knowing what goes on and what the true climate is. Only too often I have found the attitude described, and too often there is widespread discontentment and negativity.

People have not felt needed or cared about, and consequently, in many instances, have adopted almost an attitude of passive resistance. They are demotivated, and will block any impending change, do the minimum to get by, and adopt a 'me-versus-them' mentality. It is my perception that this attitude is widespread throughout industry. There are exceptions of course, and it is a joy to enter a workplace where there is a positive environment and constructive climate. The atmosphere is entirely different.

WHAT I UNDERSTAND TRUE MOTIVATION TO BE

At this stage I need to state that I believe that it is impossible to motivate someone else. A person can only be motivated by themselves. There is really no such thing as external motivation. All true motivation must come from within if it is to be lasting and of value. Sometimes we may see temporary change take place through motivation by fear, for instance through the fear of loss of one's position in the company, status, privileges, rewards or even of one's job. However this apparent change or motivation to perform better is usually short-lived. As soon as the heat is off and the dust has settled, the person usually reverts to performing or acting as they did before. Nothing has really changed, least of all the person's motivation to change. Lasting and worthwhile motivation can only come from within. This is the only sort which is worth having, and which will bring about permanent change.

The most we can do is to set a *positive climate for self-motivation* through such means as good, free-flowing and open communication, showing genuine interest and concern for the person, and establishing a stimulating and positive working environment which recognises and encourages success. The personal pay-offs must be such that everyone wants to perform better. When I talk about personal pay-offs, I am not just referring to the monetary and tangible rewards, important though these things are. A happy working environment, feeling an important part of a highly motivated close-knit team, being valued for oneself and the work one does are just as important. Creating the right climate so that the person wants to perform well because of the feelings of personal satisfaction and fulfilment they receive through doing so, is, I believe, the greatest motivational factor of the lot.

So throughout this book, when I talk about motivating people to perform well (or better), I am referring to internal motivation, and to creating the right climate in which this is most likely to occur.

CREATE A POSITIVE WORKING ENVIRONMENT

It takes some effort (but in reality very little) to create a positive and happy working environment. I believe that most of the responsibility for creating this climate rests squarely on the shoulders of those at senior and upper-middle management levels. If they were to put as much planning and commitment into making their people feel important and valued as they do into increasing productivity and efficiency, they would, I believe, rapidly achieve results. People need to feel they are valued and valuable members of the team. Of course some organisations, who already have the horse before the cart, recognise this and are already putting it into practice extraordinarily well.

Sometimes it pays to stop and ask the question 'How is it that some organisations manage to hold their key people for six, ten, fifteen years or more?' Talented people will not stay with an organisation for that long unless it is 'doing it right'. It could be argued that people are sometimes staying because of our present economically stressful times. However, I'm thinking of those times when things were good economically and it was easy to change one's job. Within certain organisations people still stayed for long periods of time. If we are to find the answers we must ask why.

Another revealing question is this: why do people in some organisations willingly work to maximum capacity on an ongoing basis? So much so that, in fact, any responsible employer will start setting limits for them and *make* them take holidays, teabreaks, and finish at reasonable times. These workers are so committed to their jobs and derive so much satisfaction from them that they give of their all unstintingly and do not hold back. We have frequently experienced this situation in our small organisation, and I have observed it in some others. These things do not happen by chance. They are an indication of an inspiring and a positive climate.

Perhaps you think that I am holding up an impossible ideal. Not so! However, it demands some re-thinking, a commitment to people's welfare, better training of managers and those in authority, and an overall change of attitude, starting at the top and eventually reaching all strata. These things are not impossible to achieve: they do, however, take thought, planning and commitment. The long-term advantages and pay-offs, as any thinking person will realise, are incalculable. If we want satisfied, loyal and hardworking people in the workforce we have to work for it. These things do not occur by themselves.

This book won't provide all the answers, but hopefully it will prove a starting point and may provide a few pertinent ideas on which an organisation can build to bring about necessary change. Generally, change happens in the following order. Top management decides the policy and sets the tone for a more positive and caring working environment. Upper and mid-management then implements this policy and carries it through. Everybody must clearly understand what the aim is of course, and communication is needed regarding this. Every leader, every manager (even those in charge of only one other person) must then be trained, and encouraged to follow through with this new policy. Supervision and discussion on an ongoing basis is obviously essential here. It may take some months before a new and positive climate is observed, but if employees at all levels are determined to create this more constructive and caring climate, *it will happen.* I have seen it happen where there is determination that it should — and have witnessed the ensuing results.

SOME COMMENTS FROM THREE ORGANISATIONS

I'm not working for a very switched-on organisation, and I personally don't feel very motivated to work well. In fact my work seems to be rather directionless. I just sort of drift along and work on a day-to-day basis, meeting the needs as they are presented. It's not very inspiring.

Nobody ever talks to me about my work goals and my role. In fact I've never had a job specification so I just do whatever is put in front of me and what needs to be done each day. I guess if the firm doesn't seem to have particular goals they are aiming for they can hardly give me personal goals to aim for. If this is all they want of me I'm prepared to do it, but I'm disappointed and I know I could do better. Though with this firm I must admit I ask myself what's the use and what's the point? (A staff member, Organisation A.)

I don't know about these people. They seem to have such a laissez-faire *attitude. They clock-watch, they can't wait to get away. You see them packing up a quarter of an hour before the workday is finished. They don't seem to have any motivation and certainly very little loyalty to our organisation or commitment to their work. It was different when I started out. Work meant work then, but that's not my experience of the average worker nowadays, or at least the ones working for us, and we would employ maybe two hundred people in our manufacturing business. They haven't got any get-up-and-go or enthusiasm. Most of them seem to be singularly lacking in motivation or ambition. I know we could do better, and we could have increased productivity. After all we've got the latest technology and equipment. The breakdown certainly lies in our human resources.* (A senior manager of the same firm.)

I'm brassed off with this company and the sooner I can move on the better. They don't give a stuff about their people, they just use us and extract the most from us, and when it suits them, discard us. I don't feel I owe them any loyalty. Now I'll be honest about it — I'm not committed to my work and I don't work as hard as I could. Would you when you know you are regarded just as a resource to extract the most from and to be discarded if and when it suits? I don't trust them so I'm not going to bust a gut for them. Why should I? (A staff member, Organisation B.)

Honestly, it's like trying to drive a ship without an engine, or push water uphill, trying to get a good day's work out of these people. We are a software business, and in this present economic climate it's pretty tough and we've got to have enthusiastic, committed workers if we're to stay in business, let alone make progress. I feel I've done all I can to motivate these people. I've kept up with technology and given them all the latest equipment to work with. I pay them good money, what else do they want? I'm not prepared to spoon-feed them. If I get one good worker in ten I count myself lucky. I don't know where the answer lies, but I'm sick of trying to get motivation and enthusiasm. I can't see anyone in this bunch worth promoting so I guess when I need a couple of new managers — which I will do shortly — I will have to advertise outside of the company for them, which is a pity. (A manager of the same firm.)

I've had three new managers in twenty months, and they've all been very poor managers. One was very slipshod and indecisive and didn't seem to know what he was doing. One was borderline aggressive and really was like a schoolboy bully in a manager's clothing, and the third was a panic artist; when the pressure was on, boy, would he panic, and when he did he'd shout at people and blame them. Why this firm employs or promotes dolts like this to be manager I'll never know. Frankly I didn't have confidence in any of them and used to just do my own thing anyway. There's no team spirit here and we seem to be pulling in different directions. Sometimes I feel that the departments of our foodchain are rivals with each other, and it's so bad, in fact, that they hug information to themselves and don't bother to pass on the information that other departments need to function well. There's no pulling together and no such thing as working together to achieve the same objective. We all just do our own thing and there's no interdepartmental communication or any focus. I sometimes wonder why I stay, but I know the job now and it's fairly easy, so I just coast along and do what I need to to get by. I don't feel any particular loyalty to the firm and certainly not to the incompetent managers that keep being appointed to this department. When the moment's right I'll move on, but in the meantime I'll use this show just as they are using me. (A staff member, Organisation C.)

I am well aware of the problems but simply don't have the time at this point to address them. We're obviously not training our managers well enough and equipping them to have the management skills they need to pull the team together as a cohesive unit, and also motivate people to perform well. However I'm already working twelve-hour days. Retraining our managers in people and motivational skills is not at the top of the list. We have other priorities. I simply do not have the time or mental energy to organise a programme to do this at this time, though I know it is needed and will have to be addressed in the not too far distant future. Frankly I'm appalled at the quality of manager we are promoting, and this is an area I am *going to look into almost immediately. I think we need to reassess our selection programme and give serious consideration to what we* do *expect in a leader. I blame the managers for the slack and inefficient way in which about 70 percent of our personnel are functioning. I know they give the minimum and couldn't care less about doing a good day's work. It's all take and me, me, me. They appear to be singularly unmotivated and uncaring about the quality of the work they do.*

With good leadership this shouldn't happen. With a manager who knows their stuff and can pull the best from people and motivate them, one should see a high standard of performance all round. More than that in fact, there should be team bonding and a strong impetus to do better and keep doing better. There is at present no satisfaction and pride in their work, and while these people must take some responsibility themselves, at the same time I do believe that to a large extent the buck stops with the manager. What I have described is the result of poor and inexperienced leadership. As you can see I am very aware of the problems and the cause of them, even though I cannot at this stage implement in-depth corrective procedures. (A senior manager within the same organisation.)

THERE ARE TWO SIDES TO THE PROBLEM — BUT WHO'S IN THE DRIVING SEAT?

I do not believe that the problem of demotivated, uncommitted people in the workforce is one-sided. Undoubtedly there are people who will never respond, no matter what good leadership and motivational skills they are exposed to. A certain percentage of people are too far down the track as it were, and are highly unlikely to change their attitude and become enthusiastic about the job they do or feel motivated about doing it well.

There are, however, a large number of people in the workforce who have the potential to become highly motivated, enthusiastic, and committed to doing what they do extremely well. These are the people I am concerned with, as they will respond to their full potential, given the right leadership and treatment. There are also many who, with a little encouragement, training and guidance, have the capability of becoming the future leaders in their organisation. While there is no strong foundation of these potential managers/leaders within the organisation, it will always be weak, and with an uncertain future.

A third group in the workforce consists of those people who are already deriving satisfaction and fulfilment from their work and who always seek to do their best. These people require little motivation — they already have it within. Nevertheless, the principles and guidelines given, if consistently applied, should motivate them to still further excellence in their overall performance, and this book is written with them in mind as well.

My experience, however, has led me to believe that by far the largest target group are those who, with inspired leadership, would reach much greater levels of performance. Too often individuals who have ability stay stuck right where they are through lack of guidance and decisive, caring leadership. What a waste — both for themselves and for the organisation they belong to!

In the following chapters we shall explore some of the answers and possible solutions to these problems. Good leadership qualities, effective communication, the ability to motivate people, decisiveness and direction are just a few of the components essential to being an effective leader and motivator — one who gets results and inspires people to keep giving of their best, and who knows how to tap into the strength of the individual.

TO SUM UP

Every day we are given stones
But what do we build?
Is it a bridge or is it a wall?
(H. Jackson Brown Jnr)

CHAPTER TWO

Strengths in leadership

Tim prided himself on his strong leadership. He saw himself as a straight shooter, nobody's fool, a man who knew where he was going, knew what he wanted and was going to get it. And if a few egos were bruised, or a few people upset on the way, well that was the name of the game. His favourite saying was 'People know where they are with me, and they know I expect to get results. I don't pussyfoot around.'

He had at times been called aggressive; this didn't upset him in the least, as he saw it as a virtue and was secretly rather proud of the fact that people saw him as a tough cookie. What Tim didn't know was that he was generally despised for his unnecessarily aggressive approach, which bordered at times on ruthlessness. He commanded little or no respect from the many people working under him on the retail side of his company's officeware business. He was, in fact, disliked by many of them.

Tim didn't know the meaning of the words kindness, fairness, consideration and courtesy, let alone sensitivity to other people's rights and feelings; what's more he wasn't interested in knowing. For a 'strong' leader he displayed many weaknesses (which other people were only too aware of), not the least of which was his habit of playing favourites. Had anyone been brave enough to accuse Tim of playing favourites he would of course have hotly denied it. The general office joke was 'So-and-so is Tim's man of the moment'. It wasn't very often that this saying was applied to women because Tim was chauvinistic in the extreme. He tolerated women but did not respect their business acumen or ability very much. He was markedly ill at ease with the female colleagues at his own level within the organisation.

Tim's 'man of the moment' was often the newest member of the organisation who was therefore under Tim for overall supervision and training for a while. Or else it would be someone who was a good athlete, and who would talk athletics with Tim (who prided himself on being a bit of an athlete). Tim would favour and encourage this person for a time, seeming to be willing to push them up the ladder quickly. If he really got on with them he would tend to promote them sooner than they were actually ready for it.

The hot favourite, however, usually became fairly quickly disillusioned because Tim's interest and backing never lasted for any length of time; usually not more than a few months at the outside. Suddenly finding he was out of favour (often for reasons he did not understand), he would begin to see the other side of Tim, which was all too well known to the rest of the organisation. The bullying and aggression that Tim would dish out for no apparent reason would confuse and shatter the 'out of favour' man of the month.

This sudden switch and change of treatment could happen simply because the newcomer had disagreed with Tim on something, or had put forward an opposing viewpoint in a meeting; there was no rhyme or logic as to why and when it happened. And so another casualty was added to Tim's growing list. The other people in the office wouldn't exactly say 'I told you so', though knowing looks would be directed the unfortunate's way, because while this person was hot favourite they did not usually trust him too much, or endeavour to get close to him, in case he inadvertently let drop to Tim something which would be to their disadvantage.

Tim didn't forget either, or let bygones be bygones. He would mentally wipe the former favourite, regardless of how well he or she performed from that point on. The standing joke within the organisation concerned joining the club of Tim's ex-favourites.

And so Tim continues on his path of so-called strong leadership, bullying and being aggressive when and where it suits him, and consistently alienating people.

Why does he hold his position, then? You may well ask. Surely management knows what he is like and the effect he is having on people? The reason he holds his position is because he is extremely efficient in the task-oriented side of his work. And yes, management does know the effect he is having on people, but for various reasons it suits them (in the short term) to turn a blind eye to what he is doing. Which says a lot about the particular top management within this organisation. For an explanation see the quote below from one of the senior managers heading this organisation. However, although Tim does not yet know it, crunch time is coming.

COMMENTS FROM SOME OF TIM'S COLLEAGUES

I have become totally demotivated working for this firm, which is a pity because I started off willing to do my best, and with high ambitions. However due to Tim's attitude and treatment of me, and the way the organisation generally doesn't seem to care about its people, I now couldn't give a stuff. I'll be honest, I only turn up to work so that I can collect my pay every Thursday. Sure I'll do what I have to, to hold my job, but I no longer care and I won't do anything extra or make an effort if I don't have to. I'm also disillusioned with management because they make little or no effort to control Tim, and they know what he's doing. (A staff member working under Tim.)

Yes, we know Tim's people skills are very poor and that he isn't liked much. However he is very efficient at his work, he's a clued-up guy and he gets the results we want when we put the screws on him, even if he does alienate a lot of his staff in the process. We are aware that this is a short-term policy and that he's only making them perform because he's cracking the whip, but in the meantime he's delivering the goods when we pressure him to. We've discussed his attitude towards his people and the fact that he kills their motivation. We know that in the long-term we're going to have to do something about it. However we'll ride with it in the next little while and see what develops. Of course if we got serious ructions among the staff or a number of them wanted to leave, I guess we'd have to look at the situation again — and pretty quickly. (The senior manager over Tim.)

WHAT IS STRENGTH?

Perhaps the most important quality of a good leader (and motivator) is strength. Often this word is misunderstood. People may see strength as a cover for aggression, hardness and inflexibility. It is nothing of the sort. True strength certainly consists in being firm when necessary, setting limits where appropriate, being consistent and not giving in to pressure — but it is much more than this. It is also having the ability to be compassionate, caring, and considerate of others' rights and feelings. Good leaders will not only display qualities of quiet firmness and sureness in the way they interact with others, but will also show above average sensitivity to the feelings and circumstances of others.

The truly strong person does not need to put up an aggressive front. The air of calmness and stability which they exude comes from their own inner security and knowledge of themselves — and what is. Those who mistakenly see strength as being tough and inflexible at all times are merely putting up a hard shell to cover for their own low self-esteem and lack of inner security. They are not confident and sure of themselves, so they need to present as always being right, knowing it all, being tough and uncompromising. Consequently they are often 'rough' on people. They defeat their own purpose in the end, for they do not inspire confidence and feelings of security in others. Quite the reverse — in fact people may fear them and perform only out of the motive of fear of loss of job, promotion, status or whatever. This type of manager does not win people's loyalty and respect. I have seen many instances in industry of passive resistance and a begrudging 'doing the minimum to get by' as a result of this kind of leadership. In the end it is self-defeating.

THE QUALITIES OF TRUE LEADERSHIP SPEAK FOR THEMSELVES

The truly strong leader knows and acknowledges that others may well have better ideas and solutions than they have. They will encourage other people to speak up and express their thoughts, opinions and feelings about relevant matters, and will focus on building the confidence of those working for them. They are committed to the welfare of their staff as well as to achieving maximum results, and people know it. This doesn't have to be stated because their actions and attitudes show it in everything they say and do. With this quiet, confident type of leadership, people are more likely to feel secure, and therefore be more motivated to achieve a standard of excellence.

Such a leader is their anchorperson; they know they can rely on them. They know that their leader will not play games such as favourites, or setting one against the other. Consequently their energies are directed towards their work and not misdirected towards emotional survival. They can, in a sense, relax and focus on doing the best they can without a lot of distracting negative emotions — evoked through bad leadership — getting in the way. The successful leader creates overall a positive climate with quiet calmness, confidence and fairness, and takes a personal interest in both the person and the job they are trying to accomplish.

In such a climate morale is likely to be high. The general feeling among staff will be that here is a person on whom they can rely and trust, and who will treat them with fairness and consideration. There is, of course, an unspoken knowledge that this strong leader is no pushover, but that he or she expects people to give of their best. In the type of environment described, this is more than likely what will happen. People will *want* to 'deliver the goods' not only because of the satisfaction and sense of achievement it gives them, but also because they feel they are valued for themselves, and for the part they play within their organisation. In other words the strong leader makes them feel valued and valuable people, and not just tools to be used.

EXERCISES

1. What do you believe constitutes strength in leadership? Write a paragraph about it.

2. What do you see as the major deficiencies in Tim's leadership style?

3. What is the likely end result of this autocratic style of leadership?

4. Do you think Tim can win loyalty and support in the short term if he continues this way? What about in the long term?

5. What do you think of management's attitudes in allowing Tim to function in this way?

6. Are there any pay-offs in adopting this way of functioning? If not, why not?

7. What, in your view, are the most important features of strong leadership?

8. Can people develop these skills naturally (grow into them, as it were, from the basis of their own knowledge and experience)? Or do they have to be trained in order to acquire them? Or is a combination of both necessary?

9. State your reasons for answering questions 7 and 8 as you have.

TO SUM UP

If Tim's story sounds 'over the top' to you, let me assure you that I have come across a 'Tim' in several organisations who have called on me for help in my capacity as a human resources consultant. I have been asked (at a fairly late stage when results of this type of management were having negative effects) to try and create a more harmonious and positive climate, to help put emotionally shattered people back together again after confrontations with a 'Tim', and to see if the aggressor could be persuaded or helped to develop some better ways of dealing with people. Unbelievably, sometimes management had allowed the situation to go on for years, and had not seen fit to take action until a crisis point was reached.

To change everything, simply change your attitude.
(H. Jackson Brown Jnr)

CHAPTER THREE

To be effective you must be decisive

John was noted for his calm, positive attitude and above-average people skills. He held a middle management position in a manufacturing company and, as such, carried a lot of responsibility. A part of his job was to see that production was consistently high; this necessitated continually meeting tight deadlines, and created a lot of pressure both for himself and for his staff.

One of John's greatest strengths was his decisiveness and ability to maintain a cool head under pressure. He did not flap and panic but adopted the policy of frequently 'taking five' and thinking things through. He would then go and talk to members of his team (in small groups) and explain to them what the situation was, and why he needed them to pull out all stops one more time. He believed in firm but sensitive leadership, and because of this policy generally enlisted willing co-operation from his team of 40 people.

John was nobody's fool. He had come unstuck a few times when he was an inexperienced manager (through not having all the facts at his fingertips), so he now made sure that he always did his homework thoroughly and had all the information available to him. Only then would he make the appropriate decision and communicate what needed to be done to his staff. Because of this he was able to be decisive and came across in a confident and assured way. These characteristics gave his team confidence — confidence in him, in themselves, and in the knowledge that they could work efficiently and well to meet the particular target.

At John's tenth anniversary party at work many favourable comments were made in his honour: 'You know what you're doing and you inspire confidence in us, that is why we like working for you'; 'You don't flap and panic and cause us unnecessary stress when we're running behind target, but just quietly encourage us, and that says a helluva lot to me'; 'You're kind and approachable but you're nobody's fool and I don't think any of us here would be silly enough to try to put it across you or push you around. You're a strong leader but you're not pushy with it'. These comments were well deserved and summed up the leadership qualities that made John outstanding in his ability to get results.

John was also a good decision-maker. He recognised that not all decisions warranted an enormous amount of time and energy spent on them, and could differentiate between problems which demanded a quick assessment and decision, and those which warranted spending more time on. Lack of this ability prevents many people from becoming good decision-makers.

John had learnt to recognise when he needed to consult someone better qualified to advise him. He also had cultivated the ability to listen, and daily consulted with members of his team whose area of expertise was relevant to the problems on hand. Having made his decision he was then happy to explain to his team how he had reached it — and why he was prepared to go with this decision, at least until proved wrong.

Though he encountered some opposition to some of the decisions made, he was usually able to persuade those who were not happy about the decision to go with him in the meantime, saying that he would give them time to prove him wrong. Often there was also a promise of standing them a drink if they did. John was not inflexible, but stood by his policies and decisions until it became obvious that another tack was needed. People did not always agree with him but they always respected him; knowing that he had this respect built his confidence still further.

The managing director of the company is well aware of John's strengths and leadership qualities, and has him earmarked to fill his shoes when he retires in a few years' time. He is encouraging John to take on more and more responsibility, and is about to appoint a manager to assist him in order to 'free him up' to prepare for his future role. He is also encouraging him to take a further degree in business management at the firm's expense. At John's anniversary function the manager commented that here was a man who knew where he was going, what he was doing, and above all knew how to get along with people, and get the best from them.

COMMENTS FROM SOME OF JOHN'S COLLEAGUES

I'd do anything for John. He's a super guy to work for. He gives you confidence, but never seems to lose his cool. There always seems to be a quiet strength about him, even when he's under pressure — and he's often under pressure. I enjoy working here because of him. He creates a positive atmosphere and we are really a happy team. You can have a laugh with him, and he doesn't mind if you disagree with him either. (One of John's team members.)

John is a bit of a mentor for me. I try to emulate some of his positive qualities. I've only seen that guy rattled about four times in the ten years I've known him, and then in instances which would have had me punching somebody's lights out. What I most admire about him is the air of quiet strength and confidence he has. Because of this he really inspires and motivates his staff. I don't mind admitting I'm a bit envious of how they hold him in such high regard. I wish the environment in our place was as good as it is in his division. John's not a pushover, though. Some people have tried to have him on and get the better of him, but they have come embarrassingly unstuck at times; because they see a fairly non-aggressive sort of guy, they think he's a pushover and challenge him. But if he knows he's right, or if anybody comes on aggressive with him he shows a very, very, strong side indeed. A few people in this organisation have learnt to their cost that, though a thoroughly nice guy, John is no wimp. So yes, I know he'll end up my boss; I guess I'm a bit jealous about that, but all I can say is there's nobody I'd rather have as my boss in the future. I can't say more than that, can I? (A colleague from another division of the company.)

BE DECISIVE

Effective leaders are decisive. They know the results they want to achieve. They do their homework, and research and seek the advice of people qualified to give them the information they need, so that they can speak and act from a position of strength. They do not waffle around, or panic (and thereby panic others) when things are going wrong, but, if anything, come into their own at this time and can be seen at their best. Their calm, controlled attitude and ability to seek advice enables them to do what is needed to rectify a situation. The more difficult and traumatic it is, the calmer and more logical they seem to become. They have inner strength and draw on it. Others recognise this and take strength from their strength. This would be one of the most important attributes of the good leader: that others recognise their strength and draw from it. This in turn releases their *own* strength and ability to cope.

An important part of being decisive is having the ability to make decisions and, where appropriate, to stand firm on them. A well thought-out and planned decision should not lightly be changed, and should certainly not be changed through pressure. The decisive leader needs to know how to (and have the will to) make decisions both large and small, and having made them, stand by them unless proved wrong.

The decisive leader's ability to assess things in a clear and logical way inspires the team with confidence so that they can let go of anxiety and get on with the job, knowing that the overall direction and responsibility for achieving it lies in good hands. This is not to say that a good decision-maker does not seek the support of others or make mistakes at times. It is a poor leader indeed who always has to put up an invincible front. Those working for them see through this very quickly, and once seen through, the manager or leader will lose credibility. No, this person is strong enough to recognise their areas of weakness as well as strength.

He or she will also actively seek the opinions and support of those working for them. More than just a good listener, this leader will have an ear to the ground regarding what is going on, and what the 'feel of the place' is. Any effective leader knows the tenor of the place without being told, and is sensitive to any changes. The decisive leader listens and takes cognisance of what the team thinks, feels and wants before making a decision.

EXERCISES

1. What do you think is John's most outstanding characteristic?

2. Comparing yourself with the way John leads and manages, how do you rate?

3. What areas do you think you could improve in, given the above case history as a measuring stick?

4. How highly do you rate decisiveness in good leadership? Explain your rating.

5. Why do you think John's staff respond as well as they do to his leadership?

6. What overall long-term results will it produce?

TO SUM UP

You can consider yourself a good manager when you get superior work from average people.
(H. Jackson Brown Jnr)

CHAPTER FOUR

Sensitivity to others: old-fashioned courtesy gets results

Martha was the editor of a small town newspaper. She was extremely efficient at her job, which was why she had been appointed to this position of responsibility at the age of 32. Martha's early background experience included working as a journalist for the leading daily paper in a large city. Though showing outstanding ability and talent as a journalist, she had nevertheless been on the receiving end of some pretty tough treatment from several senior journalists and editors during this time. This experience had contributed to the hard shell she had developed and had made her rather ruthless, and certainly aggressive, in the way she handled people. She had been badly hurt a number of times during the earlier years of her career, and as a consequence was determined that nobody was going to hurt her or get the better of her again. This attitude was reflected in everything she now did, particularly when it came to the handling of her staff.

Sarcasm, put-downs and an aggressive style of questioning were Martha's forte. She was well known for being prickly and difficult to work with, and earned the nickname 'the Ice Maiden' from her colleagues and staff. Martha got offside with most of them because of her extreme insensitivity and seemingly uncaring attitude.

When one of her senior journalists, a woman named Beth, had her fourth miscarriage after trying unsuccessfully for years to have children, Martha seemed unable to handle the situation. Instead of offering sympathy and support she told Beth, 'Well, obviously it's time to forget about all this patter of little feet rubbish and focus on your career, isn't it?' Beth burst into tears and was not seen in the office for a few days. When people found out what Martha had said they gave her the cold shoulder, and for a few weeks only spoke to her when it was strictly necessary to do so.

Another instance which raised considerable ire was when she reduced her junior reporter to tears through screwing up an article she had written and throwing it in the rubbish bin, with the comment: 'That wouldn't even make a kindergarten story.' The girl's father, who was on the local town council, called to see Martha (against his daughter's wishes) and bawled her out. He said he managed a factory which employed 35 people, and he would never, no matter what quality of work they produced, put people down like that. He complained that his daughter was always coming home upset from work, as a result of Martha's overly-critical editing combined with 'sheer bloody-mindedness and pigsty manners'. He said that, as a result of the treatment his daughter was receiving, she had lost confidence and was seriously considering giving up journalism. Martha flew into a rage, telling him to mind his own business and get out of her office, but was nevertheless shaken by the incident. Instead of it making her stop and think, however, it just seemed to make her more aggressive and insensitive.

Her staff had long ago given up expecting to receive the normal courtesies people pay to one another, and they adopted a cold, hostile attitude towards Martha. Passive resistance and payback, where possible, was the name of the game in that office, and the staff had their ways of enacting this. There were always complaints about errors and service (e.g., misprints in stories and in ads, missed deadlines, and other mistakes). Instead of putting these through to the relevant people to deal with, whenever telephone calls complaining about errors and service were received the staff would, if possible, put the irate person through to Martha, often with comments such as: 'Our editor will want to hear about this,' or 'I think you need the editor to sort this one out for you.'

Though Martha complained about having these calls put through to her, she still, as often as not, received them, the staff member concerned saying, 'But they asked for you personally,' or 'They wanted to take this up with the editor, they said.' As Martha was already under enormous pressure just doing her job and meeting very tight deadlines on a continual basis, she found this additional pressure almost impossible to cope with. She began to develop symptoms of a stomach ulcer, and also found she needed to drink more and more in the evenings to unwind and relax.

The crunch came for Martha when two of her senior journalists (one of them being Beth, who had suffered the miscarriage), resigned in the same week, saying they could no longer tolerate her bad manners and boorish behaviour, and were going to become independent writers for other sources. Both gave minimal notice and Martha was left in a very difficult situation. It was not easy to find replacements at senior level in a small town; this meant that she would have to undertake a lot of the writing herself, all of which added to her pressure.

One of the departing journalists had a very heated exchange with Martha before he left. Having nothing to lose he told her exactly what he thought of her style as a manager — and of her as a person. He said that she had a major problem, and that her people skills were zilch and that she didn't seem to know the meaning of the words 'consideration for other people's rights and feelings'. He said that the staff as a whole were fed up with being treated like second-class citizens and non-persons by Martha, and that unless she took a good hard look at herself she would find herself running the newspaper on her own. He told her that she was only getting minimal co-operation from her staff and that they were deliberately making life difficult for her; but he refused to enlarge on this when she angrily questioned him about it.

Her reputation, he told her, had preceded her far and wide, beyond newspaper circles, because of the way she treated people, and if she ever lost this job he doubted if she would find it easy to get another one. He concluded by saying that she obviously needed psychiatric help, before she totally destroyed herself as well as some of the other vulnerable people who had the misfortune to work for her. All of this was too much for Martha. For the first time in many years she remained speechless, and then burst into tears.

Unfortunately, as a result of the tongue lashing she received from her departing senior, Martha has become more defensive than ever, which has manifested itself in her being even more suspicious and aggressive towards people. More withdrawn, she is obviously creating serious problems for herself, but until something drastic happens which forces Martha to look at herself and seek help, she is unlikely to change.

SOME COMMENTS FROM MARTHA'S COLLEAGUES

A senior journalist, now a sub-editor of a city newspaper, who used to work with Martha when she was a reporter for the same large city newspaper had this to say:

I know Martha well and I know about the problem with her. Word gets around in the circles we move in and her reputation is well known to many of us. Poor Martha — I know she's a bitch to work for but I can't help feeling sorry for her. I don't think the lady can help herself. Okay, I think she's singularly lacking in sensitivity and people skills, but I also know how tough she had it when she was a reporter on this newspaper. She was working for a time under an editor who wasn't much better than she was, and maybe she picked up some of her hardness and ruthlessness from him. Maybe she thinks this is how you get the best from people. I know I wouldn't dare treat my personnel the way she does, but jobs are harder to get in the country than they are in the city.

I wish the lady would get help. It's what she needs, but I doubt that she will; she's a pretty proud woman. That newspaper means everything to her. Maybe she's scared that she would lose face if it got around that she had sought professional help for her problem regarding the way she interacts with people.

Martha's secretary, who has been with the paper for many years longer than Martha has, spoke more bitterly about her:

I don't think I've ever worked for such a rude and aggressive woman. She doesn't even say good morning when she comes in — or please or thank you for anything. That's just one thing. The environment here is so bad since she came. At first we were all amazed and I guess we were all in shock as we waited for her to settle down and change, but things have just got steadily worse. We've lost some very loyal, committed and good workers under this editor, in the advertising department, editorial department, sales, printing, distribution, you name it we've lost them right across the board. Really experienced people too who are not easy to replace. I think she's dragged the newspaper down and I couldn't describe what she's done to the tone of the place. I think she's a very hurt person but still has no right to lash out at others the way she does. I'm no spring chicken and I thought this job would last me until I'm due to retire which is about in five years' time. However things are so bad here that I'm seriously considering early retirement. Hang the money, it's just not worth it.

WHAT YOU ARE IS MORE IMPORTANT THAN WHAT YOU DO

Good leaders lead by example. This means that good manners, caring and concern for others are a priority with them. They set the tone for the working environment, knowing that what they do, and the way they treat their colleagues and those they are responsible for will have an overall effect on the general working climate. Whether the environment is positive or negative, happy or unhappy, depends to a large extent on the attitude of the manager or leader.

A leader who has a general caring and concern for others will automatically treat fellow workers with courtesy and consideration On the other hand I have frequently seen people devalued through a lack of consideration and courtesy, and the end result of this is always that they become embittered and resentful. It is very difficult to get willing co-operation from people who have been treated in this way. The ill-feeling such treatment breeds tends to last a very long time, and influences people's overall loyalty and willingness to give their all to the organisation. People treated in this way will, at best, hold back on effort and commitment when the pressure is on. They will fail to make the extra effort required because of the way they have been previously treated. *People do not forget a put-down,* and you can guarantee that the chickens will always come home to roost for the person responsible.

Do not be deceived by the fact that people may not appear to care or do not react when treated with a lack of courtesy and consideration. They *do* react on the emotional level every time, but may choose not to let their feelings show. Most people have a surprisingly fragile ego, due to a basic lack of self-esteem. I can bear witness to this as a counsellor, hearing of the hurt, pain and frustration experienced by people who have been put down in one way or another in the working situation. Their self-esteem has not been high enough to handle this kind of callous treatment (or even just plain lack of good manners).

Very few people's self-esteem is, in fact, high enough for them *not* to be affected when they are treated in a negative way. If, however, they manage to disguise the fact that they are hurt, the aggressor may never know how they are feeling, but may become aware, as time passes, that they have a member of the team who has a negative attitude towards them. Often they think that this person has an attitudinal problem, whereas they themselves are the cause of the problem.

SENSITIVITY AND CARING CONTRIBUTE TO GREAT LEADERSHIP

Everyone's four basic psychological and emotional needs are to be accepted, to be affirmed, to be acknowledged and to be appreciated. (More on these four points can be found in my book *From Strength to Strength* (Reed Books).) Ordinary courtesy, consideration and plain good manners go a long way towards fulfilling a person's deep-seated needs in a positive way. The sensitive manager or leader is probably doing a great deal to meet these four psychological needs without realising it. All of this can be very simply and succinctly summed up by the golden rule: *Do unto others as you would have them do unto you.* If we live out this rule we cannot go wrong.

Sensitivity is strength. The person in a charge position who develops the gift of sensitivity has a head start in achieving the best results from his or her people. They become more aware, and develop finely honed insights as to what other people are thinking and feeling, and how to further motivate them. The insensitive leader, like a bull in a china shop, operates by the hit or miss method — sometimes what they do will motivate people but mainly it won't. It is usually mainly by chance that it does so.

We will never learn to 'read' people accurately unless we develop the gift of sensitivity. The more we develop awareness, the more we come to know how to get the best from others and allow their self-motivation to work in the most positive way. Developing this awareness and sensitivity leads to greater insights of *what is*. If there is one thing the manager or leader needs, it is the insight to encourage the most positive response from people. Usually the more emotionally mature and 'whole' a person is, the more they have developed this insight; it is extremely difficult to lead well without first being secure in oneself. This maturity of outlook cannot really be taught, however; individuals themselves must seek to become the most emotionally mature, balanced, and whole person it is possible for them to be. Whoever develops these strengths undoubtedly has a head start in leadership qualities.

It is encouraging to know, however, that with continual practice anyone can develop much greater awareness of others' needs.

EXERCISES

1. What can be done to help Martha improve her people skills, presuming she can be made to realise that she needs to do so?

2. Do you think Martha's style of leadership and way of interacting with her staff is common in industry today? Have you observed any of the effects this way of functioning/leading has on people?

3. How is your courtesy, consideration, and sensitivity towards your colleagues, both those senior to you, and people for whom you are responsible? How do you measure up in these areas?

4. How can you improve the climate in your workplace, so that people feel more valued?

TO SUM UP

There is a sequel to this case. Martha eventually had a nervous breakdown, so was forced, despite herself, to seek help. Her job has now been taken over by somebody else. With the change of editor, Beth returned to work for the paper.

Remember The Golden Rule — and remember it's your turn.
(H. Jackson Brown Jnr.)

CHAPTER FIVE

Be approachable or you'll get nowhere

Tui was the forewoman of a division of a large company which produced car engine machinery. Responsible for the overall productivity and quality control in her particular division, she had sixteen staff under her. Her job was busy and demanding, and the company she worked for prided itself on maintaining extremely high standards, and continually increasing productivity.

Tui had not received any formal leadership training; she seemed to be one of those rare people who naturally knew how to lead and motivate people. Now in her early forties, she had been promoted from the factory floor to leading hand, charge hand and then to forewoman because of her high standard of work. Her qualities of enthusiasm and commitment to her work were frequently held up as an example by managers to new staff joining the company.

Tui had been brought up in an extended family situation where there was much discussion and communication among family members — aunts, uncles, cousins and hangers-on — about all events which occurred. Perhaps it was from these origins that she developed her very real ability to communicate spontaneously and openly and to inspire other people to go along with what she believed in and wished to accomplish.

When Tui was first made forewoman of her division, things were not going well; motivation as well as production output was at an all-time low. Tui's qualities of enthusiasm and high motivation were the reason why the management bypassed more experienced and formally trained foremen/women and nominated Tui for the position. They admitted it was a bit of an experiment, but wanted to see what she could do with a department which appeared to be in the doldrums.

The first thing Tui did on appointment was to spend a few minutes chatting with her staff on an individual basis every day. This took up approximately an hour of her time — an hour which she could ill-afford, as the responsibilities she carried were heavy and she had a demanding schedule to meet. However, she realised the importance of doing so if she were to keep her finger on the pulse of things, and identify the problems which were inhibiting higher production. As she said to the foreman of another division, who asked her where she found the time to do this, 'I can't afford *not* to do so if I want to know what's going on, and get to know my people.'

Tui didn't do her walkabouts in a formal way; rather she just wandered around from bench to bench and machine to machine chatting informally to people, not necessarily about work but about personal things as well. She found that when she began a conversation on a personal level, people very often steered it towards work matters as well. Somebody would tell her that their machine was making a peculiar sound when it neared the end of its cycle, or that the safety guard was not as firm as it had been a month ago, or that they had a better idea for stacking material so that the run could be completed faster. Tui adopted the philosophy that nobody knew the job or equipment better than the person doing it or using it day in and day out. She listened when people made suggestions and came up with ideas as to how performance could be improved. She actively encouraged them to come up with ideas for improvement, saying 'Look, nobody knows your job better than you do. If you've got an idea as to how it can be done better I want to hear it. What you say is important.' With an attitude like this how could she fail?

Tui found that increasingly people were approaching her with suggestions regarding both performance and technical matters. If the suggestion seemed viable she went along with it where possible, usually stipulating that it was on a trial basis for approximately a fortnight, with the situation to be reassessed after that. Where she could not see the advantages in following through the suggestion, she would tactfully explain this but also thank them for their suggestion and encourage them to keep the ideas flowing, emphasising how much she appreciated their input and new ideas. Joking came easily to Tui, and everyone enjoyed some good-humoured teasing on her daily walkabouts.

The first indication of change in Tui's department was in the area of morale. People were obviously enjoying their work more, and seemed to be in higher spirits. There was a lot more laughter for one thing. Gradually the environment became more positive, and it became obvious that people were taking a pride in their work.

Tui's approachability and good humour were two of her major strengths. She still had a bit to learn about other leadership skills, for instance setting limits and standing firmly by them (a difficulty for her at the beginning), but her strengths outweighed her areas of weakness and carried her through until, with the help of two leadership courses, she was able to gain in confidence in these areas as well.

Meanwhile, her approachability and gift of being able to get alongside people had already brought results. Six months from the date she became forewoman, her division topped the poll in productivity and output. Tui's team was as excited as if they had all won Lotto. This achievement was repeated several times over the following year. Management was so pleased (and astonished) at the results, that they made a special presentation to Tui and her department at the end of the year Christmas function.

Tui became more motivated than ever to achieve results and went on to take a number of study courses to gain some more background knowledge. Her department is now often held up as an example in this large organisation.

SOME COMMENTS FROM TUI'S FIRM

I have fun in my department. I love working there and I'm having a ball since Tui took over. We're all friends and there don't seem to be any slackers any more — at least not many. You can talk to Tui, that's what I like about her. She's so approachable and she'll listen to you. She has a way of turning things into a joke so that you don't get your nose put out of joint if you can't get what you want, or if she's got to pull you up about something. I like that, because there's no hard feelings. She's ruined me for working under any other boss, but she's so good I'm scared they might promote her. (A staff member.)

Frankly, Tui has amazed us. This department was causing us some concern prior to her taking it over. We knew that production should have been up to a much higher level than we were seeing, but we couldn't put our finger on why this department was consistently low in our ratings. We had changed the foreman twice within the last eighteen months to see if that would solve the problem, and it didn't. It wasn't until we took a gamble on Tui and gave her the job that production not only measured up to our expectations, but shot up in a way that surprised us. We weren't too sure that we were doing the right thing because Tui has had no formal leadership training or experience, bar that of doing a number of different jobs on the factory floor. Of course she's always been a very enthusiastic and committed worker, and been quick to learn. She's been with the department for nine years now and we felt she had a good overall grasp of how things ran. Still it was a gamble. Fortunately for us it was one that paid off. We now have her earmarked for further training, and a mid-management position in the future, though I suspect we'll have some howls of outrage from her department when the time comes to promote her. (A senior manager.)

CREATING THE RIGHT CLIMATE

Approachability, as demonstrated by Tui, is one of the greatest assets the leader/manager can have. Without it, it is doubtful that a leader can get close enough to people to understand them and the way they function best.

If a leader/manager is not approachable, their team will not feel confident to be open, spontaneous and forthcoming with their thoughts, ideas and feelings. A climate of trust is the first essential. If people do not feel that they can relate comfortably to their leader then the latter will be the loser. For one thing, there will no opportunity of gaining insights into staff relations, or advance warning of underlying problems. With warning of potential danger spots, much unnecessary waste of time and energy can be averted.

Where a safe and accepting climate exists, and communication is open and freeflowing, people are not pushed into the defensive positions of either withdrawal or aggression and will be far more spontaneous and forthcoming regarding issues which are important to both parties — and to the workflow generally.

IF THE FOUNDATION IS RIGHT, IT'S RIGHT ALL THROUGH

Creating this desirable climate takes time, effort and determination; it will not happen overnight. However if good listening skills are consistently used and the manager endeavours to become open-minded and approachable, results usually follow. On the other hand, if all of this is regarded as just another technique, then obviously it will not have any lasting effect. People sense whether or not we are being sincere and genuinely interested in them. They know instinctively whether we care about them and regard them well. Putting up a false front and using a technique to get results simply does not work. The qualities I am talking about must come from within.

The first step begins with attitude. A leader/manager with a poor attitude towards people will never be effective. Being prepared to respect others and, if at all possible, to like them, valuing their contribution and treating them with fairness and consideration is not only right, it is simply good psychology. Where a person suspects that their attitude may be at fault, they must take a long, hard, inward look and ask themselves why they have a negative attitude towards others. I would suggest professional counselling as the quickest way to discover and remove blocks like this. Reading about self-esteem can also provide insights, because this is usually at the root of an inability to relate in a positive way to other people.

If I know that you have a good attitude towards me, that I am well thought of and valued, and that I will be given the opportunity to be myself (in the best sense of the word) in my working situation, I am going to be far more open and responsive towards you. I will have no reason to be otherwise because I will feel accepted and therefore valued by you. Consequently you will not put me in a defensive position where I will be wary and suspicious of your motives — and therefore will think twice about communicating with you any more than I need to.

A positive attitude is the first step. Once the ground work is laid, it is relatively easy to motivate people to give of their best. Most people want to perform well, firstly because of the personal satisfaction and fulfilment they receive through doing so, but also because they like feeling part of a cohesive team working together in harmony (and with enthusiasm) to achieve a mutual objective. In addition, because of the good relationship established with their team leader or manager and the confidence they feel in them, they will want to do their part to reach an achievable goal.

The foundation for achieving these positive end results depends upon a climate of good communication being established between leader/manager and co-workers, which will occur when that leader is open, warm and approachable.

EXERCISES

1. How do you rate your approachability?

2. How often do members of your team or staff approach you spontaneously with problems of which you were hitherto unaware? Or tell you about mistakes they have made, or ideas they have for better performance in the workplace?

3. If the answer to the above is 'not very often' you need to look to your leadership style. If these things *are* happening, you have a good leadership style and you are on the right lines. The above is a barometer as to how you are doing as a leader/manager.

4. If these things are *not* happening, what changes do you need to make to ensure that you create a climate in which they *will* begin to happen?

TO SUM UP

It all comes back to communication, doesn't it? We will next look at communication skills, but it is important that we first lay the foundation stone of a positive, safe and accepting climate, having the right attitude towards people, and being approachable, before we can effectively use practical communication skills.

If anything goes bad, I did it.
If anything goes semi-good, we did it.
If anything goes real good, then you did it.
That's all it takes to get people to win football games for you.
(H. Jackson Brown Jnr)

CHAPTER SIX

Good listening skills are a must

Dan was the administrator of a large hospital. He was known as being a very caring person who was good to his staff, and had the ability to get things done. Although he was good at his job and in the way he treated people, Dan had a major weakness — he failed to really listen to people.

A highly intelligent man who was also well read and socially aware, Dan had some very good thoughts and solutions regarding problems affecting both the workforce and society generally, and he loved nothing better than to express his opinions to anybody who had the time to listen. He was an interesting and persuasive talker and generally gathered an audience when he started expounding his theories. His likeable personality was one of his appealing traits. People were attracted to him, and at parties and social get-togethers would flock around him. Dan had so much going for him that it was a pity he limited himself so badly through a lack of listening skills. If the truth were known Dan didn't even realise he wasn't listening, he was so busy sounding forth (usually in a very interesting and stimulating way) about some topic or another.

People who approached Dan in a working situation to discuss problems usually went away with ambivalent feelings. On the one hand he was very approachable and easy to talk to, on the other they frequently left feeling vaguely dissatisfied because they felt they had not really been listened to. Usually he had not really given them the time to get out their problems before interjecting with options and possible solutions. As one person said after a discussion with Dan, 'I feel he's only got half the story and I'm not terribly happy to have him acting on my behalf in this dispute because I don't think he really understands the case.'

Dan's employee was absolutely right. Like many people do, Dan had surface listened just long enough to get the gist of the story before coming quickly in with 'Okay, this is what we're going to do ... ' As usual, he had not really listened, and did not have the full picture. While the other employee was rather hesitantly explaining the situation to him, he had been indulging in split-mind listening. One half of his mind was listening while the other half was already mentally assessing the situation and deciding the best course of action to take.

A split-mind mentality in regard to listening is all too common nowadays. People are under pressure and have enormous demands upon their time and energy, and so short-cut and try to save time by only half-listening. Often their minds are focused somewhere else for a good part of the conversation. They may switch on and off to what the person is saying like an electric light switch being operated. The result is that while they may have absorbed the more important facts, the fine-tuning of the problem or situation often eludes them.

As a result of his habit of only surface listening and then jumping to quick conclusions, Dan had made several costly mistakes in his work. He had, for instance, ordered ten computers for various departments in the hospital without really listening to what the people requesting them required of a computer. Consequently they proved to be not what was really needed for the job — and had to be returned.

On another occasion a senior staff member had come to Dan with a serious medical problem which required him to have two weeks off for treatment. After that he would be able to return to work, but would need a couple of hours off every week for ongoing medical treatment. Dan was so full of sympathy and concern for the person that, as usual, he didn't get the facts right. He organised for him to have two months off and set in motion the process of getting a replacement for the appropriate period. This enormous misunderstanding caused trauma for the person concerned, as he interpreted the move of getting a replacement as a first step in easing him out of his job.

In his position Dan was required to attend a number of meetings to solve problems and to ensure the smooth running of the hospital.

He got hold of the wrong end of the stick so many times, and made so many mistakes in activating decisions taken at these meetings, that he developed a reputation for being inefficient and 'off-track'. Such was not the case; Dan was actually very efficient *once he got his facts straight.* The trouble was that, due to his poor listening skills, he failed to get all of the facts right a large percentage of the time.

Dan has recently been rapped over the knuckles and told to get his act together or his job would be on the line. This came as a tremendous shock to him because he thought he was so popular with everybody, including his seniors, and was doing a very good job. What a pity that a person with so much potential and ability to perform well persistently undermines his performance (and ultimately himself) through his poor listening skills.

SOME COMMENTS FROM DAN'S COLLEAGUES

I like Dan. He's an awfully nice guy, and I've got a lot of time for him. But the trouble is you can't always rely on him. He so often gets hold of the wrong end of the stick in some way or another. I can't quite figure it out really; he's highly intelligent and it's not that he doesn't care — because it's obvious that he does. I now give him everything I need him to do in writing so that he is more sure of getting the message. I'd hate to see Dan go, but really, I don't know what's going to happen to him because he's made a few bad blues lately. (A senior member of Dan's staff.)

Dan is a great guy but I must admit that at times he irritates me because I know *he's not listening to me. You can see his brain racing on to something else at a rate of knots while you're trying to explain something. There's no doubt about it, he's highly intelligent, but I wish that he'd use a bit more self-discipline and try to hear what people are* really *saying.* (Another colleague.)

IN-DEPTH LISTENING

If we hope to communicate well we must first learn to listen well. Good listeners are worth their weight in gold, and are always appreciated by other people. On the other hand, people can quickly tell whether you are really listening or just surface listening, and will respond accordingly. Who wants to say anything that matters, or reveal anything of themselves to somebody whose mind is off on another tangent? Surface listening can be compared to having your mind switched on to two channels at the same time; you can't do justice to either, or absorb the content of either one properly. Such behaviour makes people wary.

The secret of being a good listener lies in the art of in-depth listening. There is a world of difference between in-depth and surface listening. One demands genuine interest, attention and concentration; the other is something you can do off the top of your head, usually while you are also thinking of other things. In-depth listening demands total concentration: the elimination as far as possible of distracting sights and sounds. It also demands that you really listen to what the other person is trying to say so that if you had to, you could fairly accurately repeat the conversation. It means not just mentally conjuring up our own counter-argument, waiting for a pause so that we can knock down the argument and present our side of things. Such lack of communication is easily recognised by other people and simply compounds the intensity of the situation, in the end producing a negative result. We owe it to people to listen to them with full concentration. In a way it's like reading between the lines of a letter — in 'listening between the lines' you are picking up a great deal more than the person is communicating to you on a verbal level. You are receiving messages from body language, expression, tone of voice and pauses; these are telling you just as much as the actual words the person is saying. We can all gain a great deal in the way of increased knowledge, perception, insight and sensitivity, from learning to listen in-depth. The rewards from taking the time and trouble to do so are enormous. We are also far more likely to get the facts right.

People will respond in a very positive way when they sense that you are really listening to them. The message comes across loud and clear: 'Here is somebody who cares about what I feel and think.' You are giving people the respect they deserve, and showing that you value them when you take the time and trouble to do this. People will want to open up to you and reveal something of themselves, because they sense your genuine interest.

The skill of in-depth listening involves giving someone else your total concentration and attention. 'I listen, but I do not hear' is a phrase which applies to many of us. There is a danger that in the hurly-burly of our fast-paced way of life, we can so easily turn into surface listeners with little or no time to really hear each other. The often quoted line ' . . . we have no time to stop and stare' could well be adapted as 'we have no time to stop and listen.' Everyone is a loser when this happens.

So the next time you catch yourself listening with only half an ear be aware of what you're doing. Recognise too that the other person probably senses very well that you are not really with them, and they may feel confused or start to withdraw from you because of the 'not really listening' signals that you are sending out.

LISTEN TO WHAT IS BEING SAID — AND TO THE FEELINGS

If somebody is expressing their feelings to us we have a responsibility to listen to them. Not to do so will have several ill effects. We risk inflaming the person's anger, or at least provoking negative feelings in them. We in effect reject them as a person by not taking account of their feelings, and fail to hear and understand the message they are trying to give us.

Feelings are a primary human response. We play a dangerous and usually destructive game if we refuse to listen to the feelings of others. It is not only fair to listen to what is being experienced at this deepest level; it is also to our advantage to do so. We will not even begin to break down the barriers and reach the person we are trying to communicate with until they feel we have listened to and accepted their feelings. This is the way to proceed if we want to achieve better relationships with others (where they also listen to and understand us), or to find solutions to problems.

We also have a right to be listened to and, if necessary, we must tell others we have this right. Unless they are prepared to listen to us, it is going to be very difficult to reach a better understanding, resolution, or any sort of compromise.

Many problems would be resolved if people would only pay each other the courtesy of using good listening skills. It is one of the best ways of building a relationship, of really coming to understand what makes someone else 'tick', and of accurately reading their feelings. It also saves much confusion and conflict in the long run. Many misunderstandings occur, just as many mistakes are made, because people fail to listen to the real message being given.

TRAIN YOURSELF TO REALLY LISTEN

You can train yourself to listen in-depth in a fairly short time if you want to, and the method is very simple. All it takes is daily practice and concentration. You learn this art in the same way as you learn and acquire any new skill: with practice and daily application. Then it becomes a habit.

THE LISTENING EXERCISE

Practise every day really listening to somebody you are talking to. Do it three or four times a day if you can, with different people. While they are talking, try to block off other sights and sounds as much as you can. Particularly, guard your own thoughts from racing on. Give your total concentration and attention — and really absorb and think about what is being said. Also be aware of the *way* they're saying it: their tone of voice, facial expression and pauses. Pretend to yourself that you have to repeat the conversation immediately afterwards. You'll be surprised at how much you absorb and remember, and how much you pick up from the unspoken messages that person is sending to you. Do so and you will 'listen between the lines'. We gain a great deal when we begin to do this. We can improve our memory and concentration, and have much better insight into other people.

EXERCISES

1. Do you find it difficult to concentrate on what people are saying and to give them your full attention? (If so, it is just a matter of practice until you master this skill, so persevere.)

2. Can you think of a time when, like Dan, surface listening

led to your getting only half the message and consequently coming unstuck?

3. Are you more of a talker or a listener?

4. What are some of the ways you can tell that someone is a surface-listener?

5. How important to you is being an in-depth listener?

6. How would you rate your listening skills on a scale of 0 to 10?

7. Does this saying apply to you: *'I listen, but I do not hear'*?

TO SUM UP

If you want to be an in-depth listener — *concentrate on the person speaking and on what they are saying!*

CHAPTER SEVEN

You won't motivate if you don't communicate

Joanna, the sales manager for a large cosmetics manufacturing company, was in charge of a team of seventeen sales reps. She had been a sales rep for many years herself, so she knew the ins and outs of the business. Her commitment to work and her ambition eventually won her the promotion to her present position, and her work was now her greatest priority in life. Such was her ambition that she put herself through a business management course while she was still a sales rep, and made it known that she was planning to take other courses which would further her career in the future. It was this, combined with her dedication to her work and attention to detail, that influenced management to appoint her to the position of sales manager.

However, in the fifteen months since taking up this position, Joanna had not lived up to their expectations. She performed her work very efficiently, as expected, and was undoubtedly one of the hardest workers in the place, but the problem lay in her lack of ability to inspire and lead her team.

Joanna had always prided herself on being a doer and not a talker, and had little time for people who 'waffled on'. Although (unlike Dan in the previous chapter) she seemed to have quite adequate listening skills, she was not able to communicate in a relaxed and confident way. She had very little to say over and above what was absolutely necessary, and was not good at drawing people out in general conversation.

Finding her not particularly easy to talk to, Joanna's staff did not bother discussing the ins and outs of their work with her unless there were serious problems. They were not enthusiastic about their work, and certainly did not receive much motivation from Joanna. In an effort to help her, one of the directors of her firm took her aside one day. 'Look Joanna, if you want to motivate people, you've first got to get alongside them. You've got to win their trust and liking — then you'll find it easier to encourage them.'

Joanna frankly didn't know what the director was talking about when he said 'get alongside' people! To her, setting target goals for her staff and rewarding their achievements should have been sufficient to get the best results from them. However this was not enough; something *was* missing. Although on the whole her team did their jobs well, the spark simply wasn't there.

Joanna's problem was her inability to communicate in an enthusiastic, relaxed and confident way. This stemmed partly from a lack of self-esteem in some areas and was proving a major handicap for her. A successful leader needs to learn how to establish a safe climate in which communication can flow in a spontaneous and natural way. He or she also needs to know how to draw people out and make them *wish* to communicate and open up in a more effective way. Her ability to be enthusiastic and put the spark back in her team would then follow. When relationships steadily build, the pathway is often cleared for people to become more self-motivated.

Joanna's firm would do well to encourage her to attend both a communication skills and a personal growth and confidence building course. This would be a very positive first step to preparing the ground for her to develop motivational skills. Joanna must learn to overcome her feelings of inadequacy in communicating by learning a few simple communication techniques. She will also have to work on building her confidence, and in order to do so should think about how she can improve her self-esteem. All true confidence must be based on a healthy self-concept and a good self-esteem. This she could improve through attending seminars, reading, listening to appropriate tapes or even getting some counselling help.

Confidence and communication go hand in hand. Improve in the one and you automatically improve in the other.

COMMENTS FROM JOANNA'S TEAM

I can't honestly say I like Joanna, although I suppose I've never got close enough to her. She has never been particularly helpful to me in my job. I just get on and do the best I can to keep things flowing along. I'd like to get more from my job and I'd like to see a more enthusiastic atmosphere around the place but I can't see this happening. Joanna's just a bit remote really. (A sales rep.)

There are some things which trouble me about this job and I wish I could feel comfortable enough with Joanna to discuss them with her. I'd really value her input and support because I know she did my job for a long time before she was promoted to sales manager. However I don't feel close enough to her to talk much to her. I wish I felt differently because with her experience she's probably got a lot to offer. I've tried to be friendly with her but I feel she just sees me as 'Sally — rep number eight'. (Another sales rep.)

CLIMATE AND ATTITUDE

The first requirement for being a good communicator lies in creating a climate in which other people feel comfortable and secure enough to want to open up and communicate with you. Establishing this climate involves such things as friendliness, warmth, being open and receptive, being non-judgemental and not critical, being sincere and genuine, and having a positive attitude towards the other person. It all starts from within.

Having the right attitude means wanting to relate to people in an open and positive way. It means liking and accepting them just as they are and not expecting them to be what they are not. It demands being tolerant of people and giving them credit for generally having good motives even if you sometimes find the things they do difficult to understand. If we cultivate this positive and tolerant attitude, and above all try to focus on the good in others, we will go a long way towards relating well to them. They in turn will sense our positive attitude and respond accordingly.

We should also never forget to what extent we reveal our attitudes non-verbally. Verbal communication comprises only a small part of our interaction with others. The rest is in our body language, eye contact and expression in our eyes, facial expression, and the general 'vibes' we send across. If we wish to establish a good rapport with people and get the best from them, we would be wise to watch our attitude. It will come through very clearly. We cannot establish a positive climate which is conducive to good communication unless our attitude is right.

PRACTICAL COMMUNICATION SKILLS

One of the secrets of being a good communicator is to make people *want to communicate with you.* This, rather than what or how much you have to say, oils the wheels of communication. By showing that you are interested in people and in what they have to say you will draw them out; this helps to keep communication alive and flowing, and opens the doors to good communication.

DRAWING PEOPLE OUT

There are three effective ways of drawing people out and encouraging them to communicate well. They are:

- asking appropriate social questions
- making your remarks and questions open-ended
- revealing yourself and your experience

If you employ these methods you need never again feel tongue-tied and embarrassed because you think you have nothing to say. With these skills at your fingertips you can handle with confidence those awkward times when you don't know what to say or when the conversation just seems to come to a halt. Remember the basic principle: people will respond if you show that you are genuinely interested in them and want to hear what they have to say.

ASKING APPROPRIATE SOCIAL QUESTIONS

Cultivating the habit of asking acceptable questions of a social nature aids communication a great deal. Obviously questions of a personal nature are out, unless the relationship is such that the other person will not take offence. The right question gets people communicating, bridges awkward gaps in conversation, and above all gets across the important message that we find this person interesting to talk to. Questions that ask for general information or invite someone's expression of opinion, such as 'How's the new computer going?' or 'What did you think of Mrs Brown's speech?' are acceptable conversation starters.

Of course, there must be a balance in conversation, a free-flow between the two parties; a satisfying conversation cannot be had by simply asking one question after another. Anybody asked four or five questions in a row begins to feel uncomfortable, as if they are being interrogated. Questions should be interspersed with other communication skills: self-revelation, open-ended remarks, evidence of listening, in order to achieve a balance in communication. We create a state of balance by being prepared to share information about ourselves, and by using open-ended questions and remarks, which are discussed below. Good conversation must be natural and spontaneous; the appropriate use of communication skills can help to make it more so.

THE ART OF PUTTING A QUESTION

There is an art to putting questions in a way which will draw the right response. If people feel pressured or threatened by questions they will be reluctant to reveal too much. Uncomfortable and defensive, they may either become aggressive and argumentative, or they may withdraw. Neither way results in productive communication. Another method of asking questions which often draws a negative result is to follow one question upon the other in rapid succession.

One must be fairly certain that the climate is right before asking direct questions of the 'why did you do it?' variety. No one likes to feel as if they are on the mat. It is better to couch the question in a more acceptable way, using a softener to precede the question, such as 'I am sure you have a very good reason for acting this way. I'd like to know what it is', or 'You were under a lot of pressure at that time, so is that the reason why you did it?' Methods like this distinguish the good communicator from the rest. The accent here is, as you can see, on making the person feel comfortable and secure enough to respond honestly and openly to the question being asked.

OPEN-ENDED REMARKS AND QUESTIONS

Open-ended remarks and questions are those that other people can respond to and build on. Single word answers can be conversation killers. We can improve on them by volunteering more information than is strictly required in order to answer a question. Instead of saying simply 'Yes I did', we could reply 'Yes I did, but in retrospect I doubt that I'd do it again'. This throws a line to the other person, who can then build on what you have said if they wish to. Another example would be 'We've got a problem. I'd value your opinion on it.' Once more, an opening is provided for further discussion. If the open-ended remarks are on a topic of interest to both, whether work-related or otherwise, the conversation should flow.

SELF-REVELATION

A very effective communication skill is that of self-revelation. When we share ourselves and our experiences in this way with other people, we are saying to them that we like them enough to allow them to know us better. It is an act of trust to let them understand more about us, and it says much to the other person.

It also gives the other permission to do the same. Knowing that we trust them to the extent that we are willing to open the door on ourselves, they are more likely to feel it is permissible and acceptable for them to do the same.

Self-revelation does not have to mean that we disclose deeply personal information; this may be an unwise thing to do. We can just as well be open about the surface things happening in our lives. The degree of disclosure depends upon the relationship with the person concerned. To somebody whom I have just met I may be very open about the car problems I had on a recent trip, but I would not tell them intimate details of my personal life. On the other hand, I may decide to disclose very deep-seated feelings about personal issues to somebody with whom I have built up a long-standing trust relationship. We are the judge of what is appropriate to reveal and when.

Self-revelation is a very effective skill when wisely used within the general framework of communication. It reflects a climate of trust and certainly encourages free-flowing communication. When used alongside the other skills described above, it proves a very effective drawing-out skill. The improved communication which results forms a springboard for motivation. If Joanna put into practice the skills listed in this chapter she would soon have the groundwork for a committed, motivated team.

EXERCISES

1. Do you feel comfortable, relaxed and confident in communicating with people?

2. How can you create a safe, positive climate in which people feel they want to communicate with you?

3. Think of someone with whom you have difficulty in communicating. How might you draw them out on a future occasion?

4. Think of someone you regard as warm and friendly. How do they convey this attitude?

5. Do you feel people relate well to you? Why? Write a paragraph regarding this.

6. How can you help people who are shy or who have difficulty in expressing their thoughts, feelings or opinions, to do so?

7. Explain how it becomes easier to motivate people once you have 'got alongside them'.

TO SUM UP

Don't be afraid to go out on a limb, that's where the fruit is.
(H. Jackson Brown Jnr)

CHAPTER EIGHT

Being passive doesn't pay

Sue was brought up to be very well mannered and compliant. The only child of parents whose elderly parents also lived in the house, she never grew accustomed to the rough and tumble, give and take, of children with siblings. With four demanding adults to please, she learnt very early in the piece to be polite and well-mannered and to agree at all times. Negative feelings were not approved of. 'Get that look off your face' was a favourite expression of her grandmother's. Consequently as an adult (and now head seamstress of a fashion manufacturing company) she was having difficulty in controlling her staff, making her wants known and getting the best from them. They saw her as 'soft', 'easy' and a weak leader. They liked her because she was so easy to get on with, but they did not respect her.

For one thing Sue was too indecisive, constantly changing her mind about the best way to do things, and causing a state of confusion among her employees. It was well known that she would go with what the last person said or thought.

Sue was 'one of the gang' and was certainly included in the general social chit-chat in the workroom, but in reality her status was little more than this. It was almost impossible for her to set limits about anything, or to stand up to anyone who pressured her. Sometimes she would try in a tentative and hesitant way to get people to perform better, or to stop the chatting and speed up their production. However her basic insecurity was such that if they registered disapproval of the way she was interacting with them, she would back off, failing to follow through with the stand she was taking. 'Oh well, just do the best you can,' she might say, or 'I suppose it will be all right if the others are happy with it too.' Consequently her team fell far short of giving of their best, and were not well motivated. They worked at whatever pace suited them.

A lack of confidence also made it very difficult for Sue to give criticism. When pressured by her manager to criticise somebody's work she would go through agonies beforehand as to how to approach them and what to say. Often she would end the discussion with 'Oh well, just do the best you can, won't you.' The person being criticised would listen to Sue but then usually discount what she had said, guessing that she had been pressured from above to say it. Sue's section was notorious for always running behind deadlines and holding up the rest of the production line. The only time they seriously settled down to work was when the head of the organisation came in to put pressure on them. This resulted in a temporary response, but generally caused much resentment.

Sue's style was typical of the passive person who wants to be liked and approved of at all costs. Usually because of childhood conditioning, passive people have great difficulty in standing firm on issues and will avoid confrontation if at all possible. Passive people may be accepted because they are easy to get on with and are usually malleable, but overall they are certainly not respected. Because of their indecisiveness they often fail to have good long-term relationships with other people. Others often find them wishy-washy and ineffectual. They would usually rather be followers than leaders, because leadership demands responsibility, decision-making, and sometimes standing alone against the popular wish, and to do so can be threatening to them.

SOME COMMENTS ON SUE'S LEADERSHIP

I like working here because I've got a close circle of friends and Sue is so easy to get on with. Though she's my boss you wouldn't know it — she's just one of the girls, and she never gives us any trouble, I'll say that for her. Mind you, I think we get away with being a bit lazy, and things can be a bit slack. Sue's not much good if the pressure's on either or if things start to go wrong. Usually we either have to decide what to do ourselves, or someone senior to her comes in and spits a bit of fire around; then everybody sits up and takes notice.

I suppose the thing that bugs me most with her is her

indecisiveness. She can't make up her mind about anything or stick to it for more than two minutes. You don't quite know where you are with a person like that. Still, this is a pleasant enough job so I haven't got too much to complain about. (A member of Sue's team.)

I think now we made a mistake in putting Sue in a leadership position. She's a very nice person but far too weak and indecisive. She allows things to get out of control and lets mistakes pile up, then panics and stresses herself out trying to put things right. I've seen her redo the work of other people, which is ridiculous for somebody in her position. She should have had them redo it and criticised them for poor workmanship in the first place. I'm quite sure that Sue would have been demoted or fired by now if it hadn't been for the family connection. (Sue's immediate manager.)

PASSIVE BEHAVIOUR

The passive person is usually under a lot of stress simply because they are not really being themselves, but are all the time conforming to someone else's expectations. Deep-seated insecurity, combined often with a very controlled upbringing, leads them to be always seeking to please and anxious to avoid confrontation. In the process they become fragmented, losing their sense of self. Other people detect this and the passive person loses credibility.

It is important for everybody, but especially those in a leadership position, to realise that *we teach people how to treat us*. People will respond according to the messages that we are continually sending out, and therefore it is important that we be honest and consistent in what we say and do. Only this way will we gain sufficient respect to be able to lead others.

Those in authority over Sue must take some responsibility for the results they are now seeing with her. Obviously they should have dealt with this problem much earlier on and should have insisted that Sue take an assertiveness course to learn how to cope. In such a course she would learn to treat others in a more positive way, and set limits when appropriate. She would be encouraged to communicate her real feelings and thoughts and to stand up for her rights, above all learning to say 'no' where a refusal is called for. Many managers or leaders like Sue would benefit from taking a responsible self-assertion course. It would give them the skills and the confidence to do their job more efficiently, and therefore to be more effective in their role.

Management would need to give Sue adequate support while she was acquiring and applying her new skills. Other people, especially those working under her, would initially find Sue's new assertiveness hard to take. However, if Sue consistently acted in a more assertive way towards them, they would eventually adapt to her new mode of functioning and would come to value and respect her more. As the problem has been let go for so long it is obviously going to take some time for Sue to correct the situation; her only hope of doing so is to become more assertive.

INDECISIVENESS

One of the chief characteristics of passive behaviour is indecisiveness. The indecisive leader always has problems and these problems relate both to themselves and to those who work for them. They waste time and energy changing their mind from one moment to the next, and are likely to respond in favour of the person who last puts pressure upon them. Others feel confused by their leadership style, and are consequently stressed and insecure. The lack of direction from the passive, indecisive leader is not conducive to creating an efficient working environment, and can result in chaos all round.

An indecisive leader is afraid of making decisions in case they are wrong. They are also afraid of taking a stand and maintaining it until it is proved that they have a better option and are anxious about confronting opposition to their actions; they would much prefer to fence-sit because it is safer this way.

Although assertiveness training will help to overcome problems of indecisiveness, it is necessary at the same time for those supervising the manager or leader to provide encouragement and support. Initially it may be necessary to help them explore their options, decide which is the best one to take, and then to stand firm in implementing it. The supervisor should not allow them to avoid making decisions or to change them once made (unless for a very good reason). It is important to build up such a person's confidence and to encourage and affirm them when they make a decision and follow it through.

The indecisive leader also needs to be reassured that it is not the end of the world if they make a mistake. They need to know that the making of mistakes is an indispensable part of learning, indicating growth and movement. Once reassured in this way, and with ongoing encouragement and support, the reluctant leader should begin to respond more positively regarding decision-making. They should also grow in confidence and assertiveness.

MAKING QUICK DECISIONS

When confronted with the smaller day-to-day decisions which require a quick answer it is useful to quickly assess the total situation, then to ask oneself — what is the most practical and positive thing to do in the circumstances? Many times it is appropriate to proceed to do just that without wasting too much time or energy. It is important to stay with this decision until a better option presents itself — or until one is proved to be wrong.

Any experienced manager will recognise that not all problems demand the same amount of thinking, energy and commitment (we'd soon burn ourselves out if we applied these to the same degree to all problems both large and small). Therefore a quick decision based on knowledge, experience and the circumstances at the time is often all that is called for. Obviously if the problem is outside the manager's range of previous experience they should seek advice before committing themselves to a particular course of action.

MAKING BIGGER AND MORE IMPORTANT DECISIONS

The making of bigger and more important decisions is a different ball game altogether. The process is different and the quick-fix answer will not do. If we apply quick-fix solutions to these larger issues we will invariably come unstuck a little way further down the track.

The first thing is to do one's homework. This involves fact-finding and general assessment of the situation. We should if at all possible put off making any decision until we have sufficient information available to us.

The next step is to discuss the issue with people whose judgement we trust and respect — not necessarily those who are going to be in agreement with us, but people who can broaden our perspective and thinking. Having done this, it is then useful to write down what we know about the situation. There is a very positive principle involved here: get it on paper and it starts to come clear. So perhaps a mind-mapping exercise is called for. Start at a central point (the problem) and draw arms out from this, each arm representing a different aspect of the problem. We can then give each arm branches and write down all of the components of the problem along the branches of the individual arms, each with its own heading.

Another method is to simply draw a number of columns, giving each column a heading relating to the action proposed. There is usually a choice of options available.

Then list all of the pros and cons or advantages and disadvantages (whichever is most appropriate) down each column. There may be six different options for resolving this problem. By seeing each listed separately with its own pros and cons, one can often see the best option very clearly. Sometimes this can appear obvious even before all of the options are listed.

Both methods of problem-solving and arriving at a decision are effective if followed through in this way. Either method is useful for somebody who has difficulty with decision-making.

As a final check (presuming the matter is an important one) it is useful once more to run the final conclusion past somebody who is more experienced or is more of an expert in the field. Then allow a little time to elapse before making the final decision, if possible. There is great value in sleeping on the problem and letting it rest in the subconscious for a few nights before finally opting for a particular course of action. Often a little space between time spent working on the problem and the making of the decision can be of great value.

USE THE SUBCONSCIOUS FOR PROBLEM-SOLVING AND DECISION-MAKING

Let us not underestimate the power of the subconscious mind. Once we turn a problem over to it and then relax, putting it aside for a few days, we give the subconscious the opportunity to work on a problem in a much fuller way than the conscious brain is able to do. It may well be that after this time a much clearer insight can be achieved. Things which had not previously been considered may well come to mind and may influence the final decision. The trick is to *let the mind do its work without harassing it,* once the problem has been fed in. This means letting go of the problem for a period of time, and trusting the fuller brain to come up with a more complete answer.

Sometimes a flash of inspiration will come, or new insight will be gleaned which alters everything. At other times the decision-maker will simply find that the course of action they had partially decided on seems more and more to be the option they should take. Either way there is nothing to lose and a lot to be gained by allowing time for confirmation or otherwise of the chosen course of action.

BETTER TO BE WRONG THAN INEFFECTIVE

In many instances it is better for the passive person to make a wrong decision rather than no decision, as they will learn from making wrong decisions and will therefore become better at the process. If they avoid decision-making through fear of being wrong, then they will never develop the required confidence and ability. And if there is one thing a leader needs, it is the ability to make decisions and then implement them. We can only improve in decision-making by making decisions.

If Sue could learn to be more decisive and assertive, she would find that she would rapidly gain in confidence. She would also be taken more seriously by her staff and gain their respect. By risking their disapproval she will win a new kind of approval and be an effective leader.

EXERCISES

1. Do you recognise any of the features of the passive person in your own behaviour?

2. Think back to some recent decisions you have made. Were they easy for you? What process did you go through to make them? How were the decisions implemented?

3. In view of what you have read, what can you do to make decisions more easily?

4. Do you have the ability to set your limits and stand firm (even in the face of pressure) when necessary?

5. Do you frequently experience stress symptoms because you have not been able to express what you really wanted to say, and consequently are frustrated because of this? (If the answer is 'yes' then you are definitely being too passive.)

6. Can you recall times when you have confronted people when it was appropriate and necessary for you to do so?

7. If the above answers indicate that you are falling into the passive category, why do you think you are like this? (This question demands some soul-searching.)

8. Do you think other people know where they are with you, and can rely on and trust you?

9. We teach people how to treat us. Have you taught people to treat you in the right way? Do they take you seriously and treat you with respect?

10. If Sue's behaviour sounds very much like your own, would you consider taking assertiveness training to help you function in a better way and gain more confidence?

TO SUM UP

There are degrees of passivity, just as there are degrees of manipulative, assertive or aggressive behaviour. A person may be mildly passive, avoiding confrontation if they can, or strongly passive — never being able say 'no'. It is important to recognise how we typically behave in our relationships with others. If we fall into the passive category, are we just inclined to take the easy way out (mildly passive)? Or are we always seeking to maintain popularity and please people (heavily passive)?

If we continually need to please we will lose our peace of mind, and in time fragment ourselves. Ultimately we can only be ourselves (while remaining tactful and considerate towards others) if we wish to maintain our mental and physical health. Furthermore, if we relate passively in work situations, we cannot lead or inspire others, or create an environment which encourages self-motivation in those around us.

CHAPTER NINE

The manipulative leader

Joel was a middle manager in a large department store which was part of a nationwide chain. He had risen very quickly in his career, largely through his charm and his ability to get along well with customers. However there was another side to Joel, which became more and more evident as he rose in his career and consequently had a greater number of staff working for him.

Joel quickly learnt to get his way through manipulation. Playing people off against one another was his game. He sometimes thought of his staff as pawns on a chess board — for example, if he moved Bernie to this position he could then justify putting Mary in his job. That meant he could have closer association with Mary because he got on better with her than he did with Bernie. If he told them both it was only a temporary move, with the aim of giving them both wider experience, he could just let things drift on until eventually they would adjust to the idea and it would become a long-term situation.

Joel, as can be seen, would much rather act in a devious way to achieve his ends than confront the issue squarely and openly. As with most manipulators, forthrightness and honesty were not his modus operandi. If he needed to use somebody else as a cover for what he wanted to do, or suggest somebody else was at fault so that he didn't have to take the blame, then he would do so. Though he had come unstuck several times in the past because of his manipulative ploys, Joel did not seem to learn and so carried on along the same destructive pathway.

Lately Joel had been feeling a little unsure of himself because his senior manager in the department store in which he worked had confronted him with facts which showed him up in a bad light.

Though Joel tried to cover for his actions by half-truths, blaming various members of his staff and making appropriate excuses, he had the feeling that his superior was seeing right through him and he did not like the feeling.

Always plausible, Joel could usually talk his way out of things or divert uncomfortable attention away from himself. This was one of the first times he had been unable to do so and it shook him a little. Like most manipulators, Joel had a vested interest in everything he did, and was not above setting people up to achieve his ends. Joel's priority was Joel, and if other people had to be sacrificed to his interests (and this included the firm he worked for) then so be it. Meanwhile he was 'Mr Nice Guy' most of the time and came across as very warm and caring. It was only when he was cornered or confronted with an unpleasant truth that people began to see a side of him they did not know existed. Then he would be vengeful, aggressive and quite capable of turning nasty. However, Joel much preferred to get his way by subtle means rather than show how he really felt.

His terminology was consistent with that of a manipulator. If he didn't like something someone was doing he would say 'Everybody feels you should . . . ,' or 'They all think . . . ,' instead of openly and honestly admitting 'I am not happy with . . . ,' or 'I would appreciate it if you would . . .' But despite his efforts at covering his back, Joel was increasingly being recognised as a manipulative person among the staff at work.

A COMMENT FROM JOEL'S WORKPLACE

When I first joined this department store I thought Joel was a super guy. He made me very welcome and was very warm and friendly, going out of his way to help me. For a while I looked up to him as an ideal manager and, in fact, I thought of him as a friend.

However over the last few years several things have happened to make me change my mind about him, and now I feel very let down by Joel. For one thing, I feel that he led me on to believe that I had a better future with this firm than I actually had. Also I have caught him out on a number of occasions telling half-truths and casting doubts on people's integrity and honesty. I now believe that Joel uses people and will manipulate them to his own ends. A few have been badly hurt by him because when they've been on the line about something, he hasn't stood by them or spoken up for them, even though he may have suggested they took the stand they did. There's been a few heads roll because of what he has done. Consequently I've lost my confidence in Joel and, frankly, I don't trust him any more. (A member of Joel's staff.)

MANIPULATORS EVENTUALLY HANG THEMSELVES

In the end manipulators will usually trip themselves up, as we can see Joel was doing. The expression 'truth will out' is very appropriate here. Once recognised as being one who indulges in this particularly destructive form of 'people games', the manipulator loses credibility and others become wary. They then have to do a lot of work on their relationships before they can again be trusted.

It is also important, when dealing with the manipulator on matters of some importance, to make sure that there is a third person present, and preferably also get it in writing. As you will recognise, it is possible to construe anything if you take what is said out of context. Even if you nod your head signifying empathetic listening while the manipulator is talking, it can later be interpreted as 'Yes, she totally agreed with everything I said and supports me in this.'

MANIPULATION CAN BE HARD TO RECOGNISE

It is often difficult to recognise when you are being manipulated because the techniques used are more subtle. Obviously it is much easier to recognise when someone is passively or aggressively responding to you.

However, while aggressive behaviour is destructive, and passive behaviour may be irritating in the extreme, manipulative behaviour can be quite dangerous in its far-reaching effects in an organisation. We all know of instances in industry where the manipulator is not happy about something, but instead of speaking up and saying so to the appropriate person in an assertive way, they take an indirect approach, planting the seeds of discontent with a number of people, and instigating dissatisfaction within small groups. Multiply this many times over and you very soon have an atmosphere of discontent and disharmony. The environment turns sour and morale becomes very low. Unfortunately it is often very difficult to identify the source of the negative climate and what is going wrong, because manipulators, being clever, will take great care to cover their tracks.

Manipulators try to get their way through indirect or even devious means. They sometimes have difficulty in saying things straight out, or in owning up to their true feelings in what they say. It is difficult to deal with them because you may not know what their true motives are; it can take time to recognise that you are being manipulated. They apply pressure, sometimes in the nicest possible way: 'You're such a darling, I know you won't mind doing this for me.' Clever manipulators know how to push the right buttons in order to achieve their end. They make it their business to know people's strengths and weaknesses and can generally sum people up fairly accurately, pulling their strings and applying persuasion or pressure as necessary to get the best results.

Manipulative people are past masters at subtle innuendos which cast doubt in people's minds, at half-truths, telling half the story and leaving the rest to people's imaginations, planting negative suggestions and stirring things up. This they can do with such friendliness and plausibility that it can take their associates quite a while to become aware of what is going on, and to lose trust in them.

Another ploy is to try to motivate people through bribes and promises: 'If you do this I won't forget it,' or 'I can promise you a bright future with this firm. You just keep on doing this little bit extra and we'll see what happens.' Very often the promises are simply not able to be fulfilled. This way of trying to motivate people can be negative and dishonest in the extreme.

It is important in dealing with manipulators that we *refuse to play any of their games.* Insist on dealing with facts, and have truthful, open dialogue in all instances. We cannot be manipulated if we act assertively and refuse to allow ourselves to *be* manipulated. If we keep confronting the manipulator with facts, it is difficult for them to continue communicating in a manipulative way. Use statements such as: 'Yes, but what you said was . . . ', or 'It didn't occur like that. What happened was . . . ' or 'Am I right in thinking you are saying . . ? ' It is always difficult for anyone to manipulate effectively if they are forced to face the facts.

Manipulators like Joel in key positions can have far-reaching negative effects and it may take time for senior management to recognise what is happening. Eventually they will of course, because the negative repercussions will usually reach proportions which make it impossible for them to ignore. At this point management usually has three options. They can confront the person (this should be done regardless), give them regular supervision (weekly) with a senior member of the staff who is aware of their weakness, and warn them that their behaviour is being closely observed. It is advisable at the same time to send them to an assertiveness training course, and also to arrange personal counselling for them. Otherwise they can be demoted or transferred to a position where they can do little harm, or, as a last option, dismissed.

EXERCISES

1. Do you recognise any of the manipulative practices described? Have you used any of them to achieve your ends? Occasionally? Often? Always?

2. If the answer to the above is often or always, why do you feel the need to indulge in this behaviour? Where does it come from? (For example, were you too pressured in childhood?) What can you do to overcome such negative practices?

3. Do you recognise this behaviour as being inferior? What is a better way of pursuing a goal?

4. Do you recognise anybody in your organisation (do not name names if discussing this with anybody else) who indulges in the practice of manipulation?

5. What effect does this person have on you? Do you trust them? How credible do you feel they are?

TO SUM UP

What we give out inevitably comes back to us — and upon us.
(Anon)

CHAPTER TEN

Aggressive behaviour always draws negative results

Zak was an executive officer with a large food processing plant. As such, he carried a huge workload and much responsibility. He was a very task-oriented person and undoubtedly a very powerful force within his organisation, but unfortunately he was almost universally disliked because of his aggressive attitude, both towards his colleagues and employees.

Zak got some things right. He was very much into team building and would set aside regular times for team-building exercises within the organisation. He also believed in frequent social interaction as a team-building activity, and would organise cricket matches, socials, group outings, etc. He was to be commended in doing this. Again, unfortunately, he usually managed to 'blow it' on the personal level by being aggressive with people — even on these occasions. He could be abusive, swear at people, use humour to make them look fools in front of their peers, and generally put people down. For example, at the cricket match he organised for the firm, he managed to ruin the tone of the day early on by making sarcastic comments to the other players on his team when they did not perform to his expectations.

With his high drive and fierce competitiveness, winning was all important to Zak, whether it was in the context of work or play. He hated to be a loser and was usually a very bad sport when he lost. As is common with a lot of aggressive people, he did not take responsibility for his defeat but blamed other people, and so once more a golden opportunity to mould the team together was lost, and a sour note introduced into what should have been a very pleasant and relaxing day for all.

People became very wary of Zak, and after a while started to hide their errors from him. They also avoided him if at all possible. This of course worked against the organisation, because serious errors occurred which ultimately cost the company tens of thousands of dollars. When they were discovered, Zak (true to form) blamed anybody and everybody who had any connection (however remote) with the event, and generally raged around the place like a roaring lion looking for victims.

If only Zak had had the intelligence and awareness to approach problems and people with a little more sensitivity and insight, he would have known about these problems at an early stage, and would therefore have been able to deal with them and possibly avert them. As it was, people were so afraid of approaching him that when there was a hint of things going wrong or mistakes were made (even minor ones), they would cover up and go to extraordinary lengths to avoid having him find out about them. Then, when Zak was left picking up the pieces at a later date he would ask, 'Why the hell didn't you tell me? We could have fixed this early on and avoided wasting all the money your mistake has cost this firm.'

One supervisor was brave enough to confront Zak, telling him that no-one had said anything earlier because he was totally unapproachable, and because he wouldn't have listened anyway. He simply would have ranted and raved in an aggressive way at them — and who was going to subject themselves to that? After this confrontation the supervisor was very soon moved out of Zak's area. Of course it was very subtly done and it appeared to be a sideways shift, but in reality everybody throughout the plant knew that Zak had demoted this man and why.

Even a general meeting of all the managers and Zak, organised to clear the air and get communication on a better footing, was blown by Zak's aggressive style. It started off well enough with Zak saying 'All right, you guys, I want to hear your gripes. I'm here to listen.' When the gripes were expressed, however, listening went out the door.

With remarks like, 'So what the hell's the matter with you that you didn't deal with this in the first place?' or 'What kind of an idiot are you that you allowed this to happen?' Zak managed to silence all opposition, and then proceeded to use this forum as an opportunity to promote his own pet theories.

Afterwards he said to the chairman, 'Well, that went well, didn't it?' This man responded by saying 'I don't think it went quite as well as you imagine, Zak. There were a lot of resentful people who left this meeting'. Zak was absolutely amazed to hear this statement, and couldn't understand it. He thought this man was just being negative.

The above is typical of Zak's management style. As is common with many aggressive people, his communication with others is mainly in the form of put-downs, using sarcasm under the guise of humour, yelling at people and bawling them out, and generally undermining their essential personhood. Sometimes he is quietly cutting and sarcastic, but more often than not delivers his ultimatums with raised voice and desk thumping. Zak is genuinely amazed if anybody refers to him as aggressive. He, on the contrary, sees himself as a strong and forceful leader who gets things done. Undoubtedly Zak does get things done, but at great cost to his organisation and to its people!

Although Zak claims to be giving other people a chance to voice their opinions, he is never interested in listening to what they have to say. He genuinely believes he knows far more than most other people, and that his decisions will be the best ones. If questioned, he responds that he has rationalised things and come to his conclusions through a process of logical thinking. In reality he allows his own feelings and prejudices to come before logic. Anyone putting forward a different opinion or a better idea is a source of annoyance to him, and he will howl them down or cut the ground from under them, using one of the destructive ploys already described.

Because of Zak's managerial style, morale is steadily decreasing in this food processing plant. Unless firm action to rectify things is taken soon, it is unlikely that the existing level of productivity and overall efficiency will be sustained for very much longer.

SOME COMMENTS ON ZAK

The only reason I can still hack this job is that my manager is a buffer between Zak and me. Personally I can't stand the man and I don't know how he got to be in the key position he is in. Sure he's good at his job and he gets results, but he's universally disliked around this place and people avoid him if at all possible. If things are going wrong we all cover it rather than risk Zak finding out about it. Even my immediate boss does this. We all dread these [Zak's] visits to this department, and do our best to keep out of his way when he periodically comes here. Really, I don't know why the guy bothers to come through at all, he never gets satisfactory answers. Well, you're not going to be upfront with a person who's either going to shout at you or make you feel an complete idiot, are you?

As for that fiasco of a meeting to sort things out, a couple of people who spoke up were so upset by the way he attacked them that they are thinking of laying a formal complaint against him with either the M.D. or the union. They are working on it now. (A member of Zak's staff.)

I have heard many times now of the growing discontent among my managers, and also from staff, regarding Zak's management. The man seems to have a real problem in dealing with people and his style is causing a lot of tension. I'm well aware of these problems, and am thinking of bringing a professional counsellor into the situation to help him change his style, and to get to the bottom of why he feels he needs to act in this way.

As it happens, the man is extremely good at the organisational side of his work. He has a good grasp of our industry and much experience in it. He is invaluable to us in so many ways and is committed to our growth and achieving our corporate goals. He has so many strengths in his work that I'm loath to take any action to restrain him. However, I suppose for the greater good of the organisation generally I'm going to have take some action. (Zak's managing director.)

WHY PEOPLE BECOME AGGRESSIVE

Aggressive behaviour may involve either physically or verbally attacking another person. The aggressive person is nearly always 'in the right', putting others down, and discounting their rights and feelings. This behaviour is used to cover feelings of inadequacy and insecurity.

Aggressive people are usually unhappy people with low self-esteem. They do not like or accept themselves (but probably would not admit it) and therefore they do not believe others could like or accept them. They tend to bulldoze other people into doing what they want, and may well ignore the limits set for self-protection. They act in this way because usually they have learnt at a very young age that the best way to survive emotionally is to be harder, smarter, and quicker than other people. Aggressive people often believe that the world is very tough and that other people's motives are suspect.

Shouting and being abusive or physically violent are not the only forms of aggressive behaviour. A person may show aggression by making cutting remarks, undermining the other person with sarcasm, holding them up to ridicule or in some way making them feel less of a person. All of this may be communicated in a very quiet, controlled way. Nonetheless it is a form of aggression.

More than even the passive or manipulative person, anyone indulging in aggression is usually a damaged personality. However, it is necessary to distinguish between the person who is aggressive by nature (a learned childhood response) and a person who just occasionally acts aggressively as a reaction to stress. Communicating with an aggressive person is a balancing act. On the one hand, we must realise that they have low self-esteem and a feeling of inadequacy, otherwise they would not feel a compulsion to act as they do. On the other, we must be aware that allowing them to act in an aggressive way towards us only reinforces this behaviour. Not to take action is to condone what they are doing. A twofold response is called for here. We should affirm, build them up and encourage them whenever possible, but always in a very genuine way and only when they are behaving acceptably. Consistently done, it conveys that we accept them as a person. I have seen positive change occur when aggressive people consistently received positive input and affirmation from people who cared enough to try to draw the best from them.

It is also necessary to act in a consistently assertive way towards the aggressive person. We should never let them take advantage of us, put us down, treat us unfairly or get away with unacceptable behaviour. To do so simply reinforces their behaviour. If they discover that bullying tactics work or that if they apply enough pressure we will buckle, they will become progressively worse. We must always be assertive with them, take control of the situation and calmly but firmly stand up to their bullying tactics. It may be necessary to tell them that their behaviour is unacceptable, or that we do not intend to allow ourselves to be verbally abused, or that they will not get anywhere with us if they try bullying tactics. Refusing to lose our cool and quietly but firmly *setting limits with them* usually works, because the aggressive person has already lost control, otherwise they would not need to act in this way. A consistently assertive response will usually win grudging respect from the aggressive person, and will quite often help them to modify their behaviour.

If everybody from the chief executive officer of this plant downwards (including colleagues and employees) treated Zak in the way suggested above, he would be forced to modify his aggressive behaviour. There is no question of the truth of the saying '*we teach people how to treat us*'. Zak also needs counselling or a course in interpersonal relationships and how to handle other people in a better way. However, improvement can certainly be accelerated if people set their limits with him, and stand firm on how they allow him to treat them.

EXERCISES

1. Are there any similarities between Zak's style of leadership and yours? (Isn't honesty hard?)

2. If your answer to (1) is yes, why do you think you feel the need to act this way?

3. In the light of what you have read, what do you need to work on to ensure that you are acting assertively but not aggressively towards people?

4. What do you think the long-term overall effects on a department (and ultimately on the organisation) would be if this style of management were used by senior people?

5. What ways of responding to aggressive behaviour can you recommend?

TO SUM UP

When a person has to resort to aggressive means of communicating their wishes and needs to others, they have chosen an inferior path. The end result almost inevitably brings negative consequences — though these may take some time to be recognised. Aggression indicates a lack of control both of the situation and of oneself. It feeds upon a fearful, non-assertive response.

If the aggressor really felt in control of both themselves and the situation, they would have no need to act in this inferior way. Aggression is always an overreaction to an event. There is no quicker way to undermine motivation, loyalty and commitment, both to the organisation and to the leaders within the organisation, than by continually indulging in aggressive behaviour. In the end it is always self-defeating.

CHAPTER ELEVEN

Assertive behaviour — the only healthy way to go

Cyril was the manager of a small furniture manufacturing business. At 39 he had been around long enough to know what worked and what didn't — though of course age is no guarantee of learning how to achieve results.

Cyril had come up the hard way and was known as a straight shooter, but for all that was a very fair-minded and compassionate man. As we will see, he exhibited many of the characteristics of the truly assertive person.

Cyril had started off in the early days working with the owner of the business in a garage behind the latter's house. Both were committed workers and had vision; theirs was a success story. Now the manager in charge of 42 people, Cyril was as committed to the business as he would have been had he owned it. He and its owner were close friends, and there was absolute trust between them. Consequently his boss left the day-to-day running of the business entirely in Cyril's hands, and came in only to make policy decisions when the need dictated. He also took overall responsibility for the organisation's financial management.

Though he had had to acquire managerial skills in a hurry to cope with the rapid expansion of the business, Cyril never lost the common touch, and was quite happy rolling up his sleeves and working alongside someone to show them a more efficient way of operating a machine, or giving a hand when the pressure was on.

Cyril had a deep-seated respect for his people and it showed. He was always available to listen to a complaint, help with a problem or give support where it was necessary. Cyril knew when to give gentle encouragement and to be supportive, but equally he knew when to stand firm and set his limits. People who had tried to pull a fast one on Cyril didn't usually repeat the exercise. He was capable of making his expectations clear in a way which did not give offence, but which allowed everybody to know exactly where they stood.

We hear a great deal about assertiveness, and many see it as an excuse for selfish, individualistic behaviour. But true assertiveness is actually about treating people fairly but with consideration standing firm and setting one's limits in a non-aggressive and fair way when it is appropriate to do so. Assertive behaviour embraces using empathetic listening skills and gently encouraging and supporting people when the need arises. It includes making one's expectations known without the need of game playing or other indirect tactics.

Cyril, like most people, did not always act assertively. When tired, unwell or stressed he could easily fall into a pattern of passive or manipulative behaviour. These are the times we all need to watch for, because at these times inferior forms of behaviour are most likely to surface, making us act in ways which we often later regret. We all tend to have a favourite, habitual pattern of functioning and if we were to monitor this over a period of time we would find which one of these behaviours predominated.

In Cyril's case, however, his predominant behaviour was assertive, which was fortunate both for himself and his workers, because it meant that he drew the best response from them. They trusted him, they knew he would treat them fairly and would stand by them when there were problems; they could rely on him to focus on solving the problems, not on blaming the person. Cyril treated everyone with respect but at the same time he demanded to be treated with respect himself. He was calm but firm, and acted in a direct manner, telling people clearly where they had gone wrong but never indulging in name-calling, shouting or sarcasm; in other words he would handle most situations assertively. He believed in acting towards others in the same way as he would like them to behave towards himself. He was known as a strong leader and one on whom they could rely, but also a person who was very approachable and ready to listen.

It is a good indication of Cyril's management style that his employees had all held their jobs for a long period of time.

SOME COMMENTS ON CYRIL'S LEADERSHIP STYLE

I like Cyril. I trust the guy and feel that I can rely on him. For him, a promise is a promise. Also he has a very direct and fair way of treating everyone, so you always know where you stand with him. No matter how busy he is, he will try to find time to listen or tell me to come back later that day when he has got time. I have enormous respect for the guy, which is why I turned down an offer of another job and chose to stay in this company. When you get a good boss like Cyril, you don't lightly jump ship. (One of Cyril's workers.)

I honestly don't know what I would do without Cyril. He has been with me since the beginning — since we were a backyard business; and he really helped me to build it up. He is great with people too, he seems to know how to get the best out of them and how to handle them. He has the ability to be firm and decisive without being hard on people and causing bad feelings. He is up front about his own thoughts, feelings and opinions, but if somebody has a better idea than his, he's ready to hear it. If he needs advice he'll ask for it even if it means asking one of his staff. Frankly he has got better people skills than I have, which is one of the reasons why I let him manage the staff, and bow out of the day-to-day running of the business. (Cyril's manager and owner of the business.)

WHAT ASSERTIVE BEHAVIOUR IS ALL ABOUT

Assertive behaviour calls forth the most positive response from people. It depends on having an attitude that is both sensitive and perceptive. Being assertive involves not only making our own feelings and expectations clear to others but respecting the rights and feelings of our associates at all times. We know how we would all like to be treated — so we should therefore endeavour to extend the same consideration to other people.

Being assertive is compatible with the best of all philosophies, including Christianity, if we expect fair treatment for ourselves and deal fairly with others. A truly assertive person is a very caring person who has other people's interests at heart, who is honest about what they think and feel, and who does not transmit conflicting messages.

When communicating with an assertive person we are left with no doubt as to their meaning; consequently we learn to trust them.

If a person is communicating assertively they will deal with issues in a factual and just way and be open in expressing their opinion. They will not act unfairly towards people who may disagree with them, by, for example, indulging in destructive criticism, put-downs, or attacking them personally. The assertive person attacks the issue and not the person. When interacting with an assertive person you feel you are truly seeing the real person within.

The assertive person will listen to you and consider what you say but will never discount your feelings, even though they may hold an opposing viewpoint. Tact and consideration go happily together; this also is the hallmark of assertiveness. The assertive person uses statements such as, 'I appreciate what you are saying, but I disagree with you because . . . ' or, 'I know you feel strongly about this, but I see it differently . . . ' or, 'I appreciate that you've tried hard, but it's not quite what I wanted . . . '

There is no need to give guidelines on how to handle or communicate with an assertive person because they will be prepared to accept you just as you are, unless you are behaving in a passive, manipulative or aggressive way. If that is the case, they will tell you how they feel about what you are doing, or the way you are communicating with them. Often this has the effect of stopping the negative or destructive behaviour and opening the way for more constructive communication. (This topic is further discussed in my book *Your Marriage Can Work.*)

THE PASSIVE – AGGRESSIVE CONTINUUM

There are four fundamental ways in which people may act towards one another: passively, assertively, manipulatively and aggressively. Passive behaviour is at one end of the spectrum while aggressive behaviour is at the other. Assertive behaviour is somewhere in the centre; a balance between passive and aggressive.

Most people will vary in their behaviour from time to time, choosing from this continuum according to the situation, but usually having a tendency to act in a particular way most of the time. For example, I may be a fairly assertive person, but when the pressure is on I may sometimes act aggressively. When confronted by certain people I may adopt a passive role; yet overall I may fall mainly into the assertive category; this is my normal pattern of functioning. If you observe your behaviour and the way you communicate with others — how you react to situations, handle stress, respond to people, etc.— you will notice a certain pattern in functioning begin to emerge. From this you will be able assess whether you mainly act in a passive, assertive, manipulative or aggressive way.

Assertive behaviour is distinguished from the others by its honesty. It is the one form of relating which does not rely on game-playing. To be assertive means to truly be yourself in all circumstances without feeling that you have to act in one of these other three inferior ways. The assertive person insists that they are treated with justice, respect and honesty in all circumstances. It is of paramount importance to them that their rights are respected. It's also very important to them that they treat others with justice, respect and honesty; respecting the rights of other people is a priority with them.

People who act in a manipulative, passive or aggressive way, on the other hand, are always indulging in people-games, and disguising their true motives. Not so the assertive person, who makes a point of communicating with others in an open, direct, honest, tactful and appropriate way. Personal integrity is all-important to them and they will act in a way which preserves their self-respect and maintains the respect of others. Sensitivity, strength, and openness are the hallmarks of the assertive manager or leader.

EXERCISES

1. What do you understand assertiveness to be?

2. Can you think of examples of people who have acted assertively in dealing with you?

3. Can you recall a situation where you feel you acted truly assertively?

4. What are the reasons Cyril's employees are happy, and what made them stay with the organisation for so long?

5. Do you think assertiveness works in all situations?

6. If not (and if you feel that it is necessary to indulge in any of the other three inferior behaviours in order to get results), why not? Give your reasons. (If your answer to question 5 was 'no', go back and re-read this chapter, thinking about it further.)

7. What do you think could be the end results of a managerial style which is assertive? passive? manipulative? aggressive?

TO SUM UP

While we may find it hard to act assertively all of the time, we should recognise that it is nevertheless the most mentally healthy and desirable behaviour of all. It is the only way of communicating which is likely to result in an on-going positive response from others. It may be easier at times to blame things on staff (act aggressively), give in for the sake of peace, or indulge in a bit of manipulation to achieve the desired result, but in the long run these behaviours result in a negative outcome. To indulge in them may be to win the battle temporarily, but ultimately it will lose the war.

Assertive behaviour is both emotionally mature and balanced, and is always positive — it usually leads to constructive decisions and actions.

CHAPTER TWELVE

Constructive criticism motivates — destructive criticism demotivates

Danielle was the office manager of a large firm of solicitors. Hers was a high-stress job entailing much responsibility. In charge of the smooth running of the office and overall workflow, as well as the quality of the work produced, she was under a lot of pressure with enormous amounts of work required behind the scenes and continuous tight deadlines to meet.

Danielle had 53 people answerable to her and she in turn was answerable to the senior partners of the firm. The most difficult of these was the firm's founder himself — a patriarchal figure who, at 80 years of age, should by rights have retired, but much to the chagrin of his senior partners, refused to do so. Tension often ran high in the firm, but Danielle usually managed to remain remarkably calm and unruffled in the face of the considerable carping and criticism (most of it unjustified) she often received.

One of Danielle's most impressive qualities was that she not only gave praise where merited by her staff, but she could give criticism in a sensitive and constructive manner as well. Her manner in dealing with her subordinates earned their respect and loyalty and, in general, her department functioned smoothly and with far less upset than may have been expected in such a tense situation.

Generally speaking the only times when the office staff reacted in a negative or angry way was when they were approached by someone in a senior position who chose to bypass Danielle and communicate directly with them. As many personnel were rather individualistic, and all of them were harassed through the inordinate demands made on their time and energy, communication did not always proceed smoothly. There were frequent flare-ups and misunderstandings. Danielle was usually able to smooth things over, but not many of the other senior personnel were as skilled in dealing with those under them.

When it was necessary for her to give criticism to anybody (and high standards were required in this firm), Danielle did so in an honest and direct way. She dealt directly with the problem but always left the person feeling intact; because of this the criticism was usually well received. Her skill in this area ensured that people not only remained motivated to give of their best workwise, but in fact usually tried even harder to deliver top quality work.

One of the more enlightened senior solicitors within the organisation recognised Danielle's ability with people, and in particular her skill of giving constructive criticism, and, pointing this out to his colleagues, he used her as an example as to the way they should *all* approach people. It was he who gave Danielle the support she needed, which in turn contributed to her getting the high results she was noted for.

COMMENTS FROM THE LAW FIRM

I don't know how Danielle puts up with the kind of pressure we put her under, but she always manages to operate with such calm confidence, and her people skills are superb. I sometimes think my colleagues and I fail to appreciate just how smoothly the office runs, and how good our support services are under Danielle's management.

People from that department do sometimes complain to me about things, but if ever they mention Danielle it's always in the most positive vein. It's not that she's too easy with them; she has high standards, is quite demanding, and when she has something to say she can say it. It's just that she seems to have the knack of taking the sting out of what she says, so that people are left feeling that they want to do better, but not being resentful of the fact that she has had to criticise their work. We are under a great deal of pressure here and frankly I think the whole place would be in a sorry state without her.

Before Danielle came we were in a state of absolute crisis. Bill, who is now our legal researcher, was managing the office, and though efficient at his work, he didn't have many clues about managing people. His idea of correcting errors or giving criticism was to read the riot act. He would leave them feeling shattered and pretty resentful, and would generally leave a lot of pieces for the rest of us to pick up. After a couple of years of Bill's administration, that whole department, which is really the ship's engine room, was disintegrating. We were losing so many good people that we had to look seriously at the situation. We decided that we had made a major error in putting Bill in a position where he was called upon to take over all control of people's performance. So we moved him into research (obviously we didn't want to lose him), and we head-hunted Danielle, because a number of us had heard of her good reputation with people. I don't think I'm exaggerating when I say that she pulled this department out of the mire just in time. So you can see why I hold her in such high esteem. (A senior partner of the firm.)

I was on the point of leaving when Danielle came. I thought, 'Oh no! Not another office manager to get used to.' But from the moment Danielle introduced herself to me I liked her, and I have grown to respect and admire her more ever since. She has a calm, authoritative air about her but she is very caring, and I would say emotionally mature. She leaves you alone to do your work and doesn't interfere as long as you are doing it satisfactorily. In fact she quickly acknowledges good performance. I like that because I've never had it before. However, you know where you are with her. She's quite frank if she's not happy with something and if your work is sub-standard she'll tell you, but in a kindly way, and you never feel you have to take it personally. The guy who managed the office before, on the other hand, used to bawl me out, usually in a loud voice and in front of everybody. I always felt it was very destructive criticism. Once he was wound up there was no stopping him and he would just yell and even thump the desk. He also attacked personally, which I did not like. I certainly could not have taken any more of him.

That's why it's so good to have somebody now who at least knows how to treat you fairly. Danielle's only fault that I can see would be that she tends to get a bit too involved with everybody, and so takes too much on board personally. Nice for us maybe, but not so good for her. (One of Danielle's staff.)

HOW TO GIVE CONSTRUCTIVE CRITICISM

Here is an outline of the six steps we can follow in trying to give criticism constructively.

- Consider an overview of the person's total performance.
- Attack the *issue,* not the *person.*
- Give the person the right of response, and listen to what they have to say.
- Invite them to come up with their own solution to the problem (which calls upon their own internal motivation).
- Firm up and reinforce the decision they have made. ('So you'll do the contracts this way in the future?')
- Finish with a positive statement which leaves them with a feeling of hope, and also, most importantly, the knowledge that they are not being personally rejected.

Let us now consider each step in greater detail.

Consider an overview of the person's total performance

It is totally unfair to focus only on the errors a person makes and to concentrate on this negative aspect of their work. We owe it to them to take into consideration how they perform overall. Take, for instance, the example of a loyal and committed worker who will go the extra mile if necessary, and who gives of their very best to the organisation, but who has problems in the area of decision-making. When discussing this area of weakness, we must also take into account their total on-the-job performance. If our criticism is to be fair and constructive, we need to balance error with overall performance, and should acknowledge the latter in the initial stages of the criticism. This does more than just ensure that we are fair, it also puts the employee in the right frame of mind to receive the criticism which is to follow, as well as helping to prevent their adopting a defensive stance (perhaps responding with either aggression or withdrawal).

Attack the issue, not the person

When it comes to actually delivering the criticism, it is very important to attack only the issue and not the person. We do not have the right to attack personally, and never more does this apply than when we are giving criticism. The criticism must be just and fair, and we must only deal with the *known facts* — not with what we presume the person's motive was in doing what they did, or in trying to interpret their feelings. (For instance, 'I don't think you had a very positive attitude towards this in the first place.') We can never presume to know what is going on inside another's head. We can only deal with what actually happened, and the way they acted. Name-calling, being abusive, attacking personally, using sarcasm or put-downs, shouting and other belligerent or negative methods of communicating are simply not acceptable.

Give the person the right of response and listen to what they have to say

It is never easy to take criticism. Consequently it is very important that the person being criticised feels that they also have a right of response, and that their reply will be listened to. With the best will in the world we may not know the full story or have all the facts. Therefore we owe them the right of reply.

It may well be that when we hear the full story we may choose to modify (or in some cases even withdraw) the criticism. We may have been fed only a very one-sided version, or it may be that we did not know of the pressures the person was under at the time.

It also makes it much easier for someone to accept criticism if they know they are being listened to, and that their actions are being fairly assessed. We owe it to them to actively listen to their side of the story, and to acknowledge it in some way.

Invite the person being criticised to come up with their own solution to the problem

Having the person decide for themselves what they can do to correct the situation is the best form of motivation. Giving them the right to decide a course of action empowers them. They now have choice, and if they choose a means of correcting the problem, they are far more likely to be well *motivated* to work at it. Internal motivation is the only sort worth having. If we suggest a course of action to them, we are motivating them externally; this is an inferior source of motivation because it is being imposed upon the person, so they are less likely to act upon it. Real change will occur only when there is self-motivation. Encouraging the person to come up with their own solution will be much more likely to bring about the changes required. Results will always be inferior if we have to impose the solution or action to be taken.

Reinforce the conclusions the person has come to

In order to clarify the situation and ensure that the employee carries through the corrective measures they say they will undertake, it is necessary to reiterate and reinforce what they have said. We need to make a statement such as, 'So, what you are going to do now is . . . ' Repeat what they have said in simple, unambiguous language so that neither of you is left in any doubt as to the corrective action to be taken. This not only ensures complete understanding on both sides, but it reinforces for the person concerned that they *need* to take action, that they *will* take action, and *what action* they will take.

If your team member seems uncertain as to what corrective measures should be put into practice, give them a little more time and ask them to get back to you with their solution. In most instances, however, they will be able to give you an answer on the spot. Reinforcing the proposed corrective measures clearly lets them know your expectation of them: that they will correct the error they have made.

Finish with a positive statement leaving the person intact, with hope, and not feeling personally rejected

We all have fragile egos, and criticism can easily leave us with a raft of negative feelings. When you criticise one of your team members they may feel that they have fallen in your estimation, that they have irrevocably blotted their copybook and that nothing they do in the future can ever rectify this. They may also feel that their future with the organisation has a big question mark over it. Such feelings of hopelessness are great demotivators, and everybody loses if one of the team is experiencing them.

We have a responsibility always to ensure that people are left not feeling destroyed after criticism, but rather feeling there is hope for improvement. Regardless of how factual the criticism is, if the person is not left feeling intact, then we have failed in our task. How well criticism is given is an indication of our communication skills. The good communicator gives criticism in such a way that there is no sting in it. The person needing correction is aware that they have been shown where they were going wrong, but it has been made very easy for them to accept, and so there are no lingering feelings of resentment. If a person is left with feelings of rejection, the criticism has been badly given. They should rather feel that they have been taught something which is of value to them, that their superior was genuinely trying to help them to improve their performance, and was in no way trying to undermine them as a person.

The giving of criticism is one of the most sensitive areas in management, and in my experience very few people do it well. Finishing the discussion on a positive note, preferably with some affirmation of the employee's worth, will guard against the negative feelings, which act as a *block* to better performance, and will provide a better climate for the development of self-motivation for improvement in the future.

EXERCISES

1. Can you think of instances where people have handled the giving of criticism well?

2. What are the benefits of giving criticism in Danielle's way, rather than Bill's? What do you think of Bill's way of giving criticism?

3. Do you agree with the statement that most people have a fragile ego, even though they may not show it?

4. How have you personally reacted when you have been on the receiving end of destructive criticism?

5. How have you reacted when you have been criticised in a constructive and sensitive way?

6. When you have been called upon to give criticism, how have you done so?

7. What is the usual reaction you receive from people whom you criticise?

8. Do you feel that you need to make any changes in your method of criticising?

TO SUM UP

A person knowing the power of his word becomes very careful of his conversation. He only has to watch the reaction of his words to know that they 'do not return void'.
(Florence Scovel Shinn)

CHAPTER THIRTEEN

How to motivate your team

Gerry was very good in his position as sales manager of a large computer software organisation. He had done extensive training in his field and there weren't too many people in the computer software business who knew more about the product than Gerry. His research and training, combined with dedication to his work, had eventually resulted in him being chosen to head the sales team.

Unfortunately, however, Gerry had not lived up to the expectations that senior management had had of him. There was no question about his own commitment and expertise, but he had not as yet shown much potential to lead. He would listen to his team's problems, give advice and help them sort out problems, but did not seem to have the ability or know-how to build team spirit, and inspire his people to do better.

Part of the problem was that Gerry was not giving each of his team (twelve people) regular ongoing supervision. When people receive regular supervision they have a framework to work within. They receive better direction, know what they should be aiming for, and have regular feedback as to how they are succeeding. They also have the opportunity of receiving ongoing support, which certainly is an important motivator in itself. If a person feels that they are supported and guided, then they are bound to feel more motivated to achieve, and it enables them to function at a better level.

Another way in which Gerry was failing to set a positive climate for self-motivation was in his own rather unemotional, low key and almost bland approach. He would transmit information, and even some expectations to his team, but without enthusiasm, and usually in a rather unimaginative way. Gerry believed that the facts should speak for themselves. It had simply not occurred to him that, if he wished to motivate people, more than just the relaying of facts might be needed.

The greatest keys in helping people to become self-motivated are imagination, enthusiasm, challenges and inspiration. People thrive on being challenged to extend on both the mental and emotional levels. The inspiring leader becomes adept at finding the key to motivating each team member from within. Dynamic leadership, where the manager or team leader is innovative, imaginative, always seeking to extend, and ready to regard obstacles as welcome challenges, will inspire others to perform at a much higher level. The leader must of course *lead from the front* and not just sit back, waiting for direction to become obvious. They need to find direction, taking into account the overall vision for the company and then challenge and inspire others to achieve the necessary goals.

Gerry was really missing out in these areas. He had a lot of knowledge but, in common with many others in management positions, did not have the skills to impart it well. Gerry needed to learn how to lead, to find a vision, to motivate people through his enthusiasm and decisiveness, and to give each member of his team regular supervision. Nobody worked harder than Gerry — that was acknowledged — but a lot of his effort and input was wasted because he was not realising and applying these simple leadership concepts.

Gerry's department did not thrive as it should have, and management were aware of it. Sales teams were sitting back, able to bring in sufficient business to keep the company ticking over, but not by any means realising their own (and consequently their organisation's) potential. At a recent meeting, senior management discussed moving Gerry to a different position within the organisation.

Aware that they may have put Gerry in a position that he is not best suited to, the senior managers at the meeting voted to give him three more months to see whether or not he could develop some real leadership qualities with some assistance. Consequently they have decided to explore what courses are available to help him in the areas in which he is lacking.

Management in this organisation must also take some of the blame in that they had not been giving Gerry regular ongoing supervision, thereby helping him to become a more dynamic leader. Nor were they giving him enough support. Within the organisation there were leaders who were noted for their effectiveness in motivating and getting the best from their team, a number of whom could have been a suitable mentor for Gerry. One suggestion which could work well (in addition to weekly supervision with a highly motivated senior manager) would be to adopt a buddy system, and get Gerry to work with another manager who is a proven leader. This could be done in a way which does not make Gerry feel inferior — for example, it could come under the heading of swapping of skills in a mutual support system.

It is a pity if somebody with Gerry's know-how, expertise and obvious potential misses out, through insufficient training and support, on becoming the inspiring leader he is capable of being.

COMMENTS FROM THE ORGANISATION

I've got a lot of respect for Gerry's knowledge and commitment to work but he's not really my idea of a leader. It's just my opinion but I believe it's more important for a manager to know how to motivate people and make them extend themselves, than it is for them to have practical knowledge of the job themselves. In the company I worked for prior to getting this job, there was a guy who really challenged me. I found that I surprised myself in how much I was able to achieve, and the funny thing about it was, though I got annoyed at times with him having such a high expectation of me, I actually quite enjoyed the challenge of having to perform better all the time. It's like my work graph was steadily going upwards, and along with it my capacity to be successful and achieve.

Most of the team like Gerry and enjoy working with him, but I'm sure they would all agree — he certainly doesn't help motivate or stimulate them to better performance. (A member of Gerry's sales team.)

We've probably been unfair to Gerry in making him sales manager without adequate training. The reason we did is because the guy is so good at his work and has such good product knowledge, along with an uncanny ability to sort out glitches that leave other people floundering. We thought that the team would learn so much from him that it would more than compensate for any lack of natural leadership qualities. I realise now that we were wrong in this. We also thought that he would grow into the job and would start to pull the team together.

Where we went wrong, I think, is in not giving him some training before we put him in the position, and also in not keeping a much closer eye on him over the two years he's been in the job. Trouble is, this is such a high pressure outfit that finding the time to help a guy like Gerry is very difficult. I accept that this is a short-sighted policy, and already in this short time period we are beginning to pay for our mistake. However, Gerry's a bit of a walking computer and we wouldn't want our rivals getting their hands on him. So for our sake as well as his, we hope that he can, with more support, prove himself as sales manager. (Gerry's senior manager.)

THE VALUE OF SUPERVISION

One of the reasons why Gerry is not giving strong and definite leadership is his failure to give regular and ongoing supervision to his sales team. Supervision has a fourfold purpose:

- It is an opportunity for the team members to *air their problems* with somebody who is more experienced than they are.

- It is a time when they can receive *support and encouragement.* This will be particularly effective if the supervisor is aware that we have certain needs — to be affirmed, accepted, appreciated and acknowledged — and that we will all do better if these needs are positively met.

- It is a time when *constructive criticism* can be given. We can all learn much from constructive criticism and through it can learn, grow, and possibly find better direction. This sort of guidance can be a positive force for motivating the team member. He or she will know that their supervisor is trying to help them, steer them in the right direction, and show them how to improve their overall performance. They will be well aware that what is said is said in a spirit of goodwill, and most people will respond positively to this. Criticism, if wisely given, can be one of the greatest learning and motivational tools there is.

- Supervision is the perfect time to look at and *review goals*. People always perform better and have clearer direction if they are identifying and reviewing goals. This is an excellent opportunity for the supervisor to help them to do so. A part of supervision should be spent in revising, reaffirming or fine-tuning their overall career aims. The supervisor should ensure that the person sets realistic stepping-stone goals (described below) on the way to achieving their main, long-term goals. Unrealistic ones will pressurise them too much and so be self-defeating. (My book *You Can Do It!* is all about goal setting and motivation, and could be a useful guide in helping people to achieve and set goals.) The very act of working on goals with a supervisor helps to keep people on track.

Supervision can be very valuable if the time is well spent and is structured. It is a time when the team member can be realistically extended, encouraged, supported, and left feeling uplifted and motivated to achieve better performance.

If Gerry were to take the time and trouble to regularly supervise his team on a one-to-one basis, he would soon find encouraging results. For one thing he would get to know each of them far better — their areas of weakness and strength, and where they needed help to do better. This would be a strong, motivating force which would result in a higher level of performance. Similarly, if Gerry himself had had the benefit of supervision, he would also be much more effective in his present role.

Supervision should be given at least fortnightly, and it should be one-to-one. It should be scheduled into diaries so that it is regarded as high priority, uninterrupted time. Where this value is placed upon it, results will almost certainly follow. If the team is too large for one person to handle all the supervision (as may well be so in Gerry's case), then other senior and experienced members of the team should be trained to help supervise. Supervisors need to be hand-picked for their skills in relating to people. They need to have some training in how to give supervision most effectively. It makes sense to delegate this important task where, because of the size of the team, it is difficult for the manager to do it all themselves. The manager/team leader should, of course, be the overall supervisor of those selected to do this important work.

STRONG, DECISIVE LEADERSHIP

Gerry was also failing to motivate people in that he was not showing the characteristics of strong, decisive leadership. The leader is the anchorperson on whom the team must be able to rely for firm guidance and decisiveness. A good leader will give team members confidence and make them feel secure. People need to know that when chaos reigns, or when things begin to go seriously awry, their leader will keep calm, stand firm and take the final responsibility. They also need to know that their leader will assess the situation and make calm, logical decisions regarding the best course of action to take. A leader who exhibits these strengths will be respected and will provide the foundation for a strongly motivated team.

ENTHUSIASM

Another area in which Gerry was deficient was in conveying enthusiasm for the goals and vision he was holding before his team members. He would outline plans and define goals for them, but would then fail to inspire his people to achieve them, partly because of his *method* of relaying the relevant information to them. Everything was delivered in a very factual way and in a deadpan voice; he was merely relaying the facts as they were, and failing to engage the imagination of his team. He overlooked one great motivational factor: the way information is presented has a big impact on the way in which it is accepted. We see things in pictures, therefore if we want to inspire and help motivate others we have to paint word pictures for them. Gerry's lack of ability to do this, plus the totally unemotive language he was using, was the cause of the problem.

Enthusiasm is one of the greatest gifts the leader/motivator can have. We first have to be enthusiastic about something ourselves before we can make others enthusiastic about it. We will never inspire or enthuse them unless we are excited, a little on a high, exhibiting a certain amount of tension and a reasonably high level of energy about the particular project we are trying to sell. And let's face it when we are trying to motivate somebody we are trying to sell something to them (even if it's only the reason why they should endeavour to perform better). All of this adds up to one thing — enthusiasm!

If we want other people to be enthusiastic and committed to anything, then we have to not only be reasonably excited about it ourselves, but translate the message to them in such a way that they catch our fire. All the great motivators in the world today will tell you that their greatest tool is enthusiasm. It is almost impossible to inspire anybody to greater heights of achievement or to give them a vision to move towards if you are not relaying the facts in an enthusiastic way; doing so brings the project or goal *to life* for them. What Gerry really needs to do is to ensure that he does this when working with his team.

IMAGINATION AS A MOTIVATIONAL TOOL

Another of the motivator's greatest tools is imagination. It fires people up and instils in them a desire to commit themselves to a certain course of action — maybe to achieve goals, change direction, perform better. In order to translate messages in an enthusiastic way to his team, Gerry needs to first use his imagination. It is very difficult for anybody to be enthusiastic unless they can visualise the results they wish to achieve. Gerry will begin to release in himself the ability to translate his message in an enthusiastic way when, and only when, he can hold in his mind's eye a picture of what he wishes his team to achieve.

If he can imagine it strongly enough, he will begin to feel it, smell it, touch it, taste it, and it will start to become a reality to him. When this happens he will automatically transmit the vision and the excitement that this vision creates to the rest of the team. Enthusiasm follows imagination. In the previous section I talked about the need for the team to catch his fire. First Gerry must stoke the fire within himself, then find ways of communicating the energy to others. He must fire their imagination. Again by painting the right word pictures he will do so.

Once feelings back up facts, things begin to happen, and what is a task to be accomplished, or a goal to be achieved, becomes a vision that must be realised at all costs. When people catch the fire and see the vision, they release in themselves drive, energy, commitment, and an overwhelming desire to proceed along the right path to make these things happen. If you can imagine that which is important for you to achieve, you will almost certainly cause other people to also tap into this valuable motivational resource. Enthusiasm and the correct use of our creative imagination go hand and hand. With it we can motivate ourselves and other people. So share your vision and set goals for the team.

VISION AND GOAL-SETTING

If we wish to help to motivate people to achieve and to be successful in reaching attainable goals, we need to give them some building blocks to work with. This is where overall vision and then goal-setting comes in. Goals are far more likely to become an achievable reality if they are fuelled with vision. *So having a vision is the first step*; it needs to be thought through, clearly defined, shared and discussed. Talking about the shared vision will lead to definition of the goals. These goals will be the practical step that will enable the company, the team, to reach the vision.

In addition to setting goals during supervision with each member of the team, Gerry should also be having team meetings in which goals for all are clearly defined. He needs to share his overall vision for what he wants for the company, for his department, and for what he wishes his team to achieve. Without having their own goals set and regularly discussed and reaffirmed, a team will lack motivation, a team spirit and can lose direction. Gerry's team was certainly beginning to lose direction (they had already lost motivation).

Once major team goals have been established, they should (as with personal goals) then be broken down into achievable stepping-stone goals. What point should we be at in achieving our major goal in six months? In three months? In one month? Stepping-stone goals are discussed at length in my book *You Can Do It!,* and some of this material is included in the pages that follow.

What tasks do we need to accomplish in order to achieve these stepping-stone goals? What milestones do we set for the individual and the team as a whole? What can we do to support each other in achieving these goals? How can we motivate each other to do so? These and other questions should be regularly explored at team meetings. Gerry would find, if he structured the team meetings to deal with these questions and others which will arise from them, and held meetings on a regular basis (preferably weekly), team members would begin to motivate each other, and enthusiasm and commitment within the team would begin to rise.

STEPPING-STONE GOALS

Once you have completed your major goal-setting exercises, it is important to break down the whole plan into manageable parts by setting intermediate stepping-stone goals to help you reach your major goals. What may seem too remote and difficult to achieve now becomes possible and attainable if viewed in workable steps. An unrealistic expectation of oneself is high on the list of reasons why people fail to reach their goals. Be prepared to go up the steps, one at a time, until you reach your chosen goal. Don't try to jump from one floor to the next — this is the guaranteed way to fail. People who try to do this usually give up in despair because they've failed so many times they can no longer bear the pain involved. They give up trying rather than face failure and disappointment yet again. Their unrealistic expectation of themselves, which can be viewed as 'too much too soon', condemns them to failure and, eventually, they sink into a state of despair and may never again risk extending themselves in order to achieve a goal. What a waste, and what a tragedy.

If all people disillusioned by their inability to achieve goals in their lives had broken them down into workable steps, going at a realistic pace, they may well have achieved success.

Another reason why people fail to achieve their goals is because they put themselves under too much stress in working to achieve them quickly. If they are doing this to themselves, you may be sure they are also doing it to other people. Some people create a state of stress wherever they go. Others resent this, and especially the effect on them personally, and so fail to support and help such people. As a result a vicious circle is set in motion: the more the person feels unsupported and isolated, the more stressed they become. This is the path to burnout with its ensuing negative effects upon everybody.

If we have realistic expectations, and steadily extend ourselves through aiming for attainable stepping-stone goals, our capabilities and potential for achievement steadily increases. These conditions give us the best chance of succeeding and eventually reaching our long-term goal. Each time we achieve a minor goal our confidence increases, and so does the chance of attaining the ultimate aim. Success consists of a series of daily extensions, which help us to achieve each of the stepping-stone goals leading to our major goal.

EXERCISE

Consider one of your major goals. Break it into manageable steps. Now build a time frame into the steps. Make it realistic and workable.

1. If you think it is going to take you ten years to achieve this major goal, break the period into sections up to the seven-and-a-half-year stage.

2. What point do you think you should be at in seven-and-a-half-years' time? In five years' time? In three years' time? Think of these points as winning posts you expect to pass along the way, defining each step in a general way.

3. Now divide your time and track rate even more exactly. Set yearly milestone goals for the first three years. What exact milestone goal would you expect to have achieved by the three-year mark? The two-year? The one-year mark?

4. Fine tune the first year to three-monthly checkpoints. Every three months during the first year assess and check your progress. Where are you on your total goal path? How far

have you progressed? Have you deviated from your course? Are you still on target to do it in time? How is your goal blueprint looking? Have these assessments caused you to reinforce or alter your total goal plan?

5. Each year repeat number 4, so that your overall plan breaks down to three-monthly checkpoints every year. And repeat number 3, so that you are setting yearly milestone goals. Your yearly or three-yearly milestone goals differ from the three-monthly checkpoints, in that the former are definite mini-goals in themselves, leading to your major goal. Think of them as milestones you hope to reach and pass by a specified time.

It is also important for you to do a written fortnightly or monthly goal-assessment check but we will deal with this later. For now, just concentrate on doing the breakdown plan of one of your major goals, as outlined. Then fill in the chart below with your conclusions. Now draw up some more charts in the same way, and use one for each of your major goals. Those who enjoy a challenge may then wish to combine all their long-term goals into one major chart.

SAMPLE CHART

MAJOR GOAL..

ESTIMATED ATTAINMENT TIME..

Stepping-stone goals

Milestones *(Write in details of your yearly milestone goals.)*	Estimated attainment time *(These times are suggestions only; adjust to suit your time frame.)*
No. 9..	9 years
No. 8..	8 years

No. 7..7 years
No. 6..6 years
No. 5..5 years
No. 4..4 years
No. 3..3 years
No. 2..2 years
No. 1..1 year

Three-monthly assessment/progress checkpoints

(Repeat each year.)

Checkpoint	Time frame
1.	3 months
2.	6 months
3.	9 months
4.	12 months

REGULAR WRITTEN GOAL CHECKS

I was once researching the factors which made particular people successful. Was there anything that these people, who came from widely differing backgrounds, had in common, that made them so outstandingly successful?

There were a few common denominators: a high standard of ethics, confidence, good communication skills, the ability to take calculated risks (and to see mistakes as stepping-stones), 'stickability', innovation, follow-through skills, vision, clearly defined goals — and regular written goal checks.

The people I researched had all formed the habit of regularly writing out their goals. Some wrote them daily, others weekly, but none less than fortnightly, and these were people who had made it to the top!

In regularly writing out our goals, we are conditioning ourselves to move steadily towards them and experience success in reaching them. We are, in essence, reinforcing them in our subconscious mind.

Many people who realise the value of writing out their goals do so weekly. If you cannot see yourself doing this, I would recommend that you make a realistic commitment to do what you know is possible and realistic for you. Think it through seriously and make a promise to yourself; one you know you're going to honour. I personally believe that a monthly commitment is the absolute minimum if any results are to be achieved. A fortnightly commitment is better. When you have made your decision, schedule it into your diary for the next year, for example, an hour on the last Friday of every month. This is the way to ensure that you stick to it.

Keeping on course with your goals is important, and is another excellent reason to write them out regularly. We need to keep checking, assessing and measuring to ensure we are going in the right direction. Life, circumstances and people change, and goals set as little as two years ago may not necessarily be the right ones now. In regularly doing this exercise, we reinforce for ourselves that we are steadily heading in the right direction without wasting any more time, energy and commitment. Remember that your two most precious commodities are yourself and your time; spend both wisely. Regularly writing out goals ensures that we are not steering in the wrong direction for any length of time. The more we write them out, the more we will be able to see whether or not we are still on the right course for our ultimate benefit and welfare.

You may also find better and more efficient ways of achieving your goal, because the act of writing triggers creative thinking, which may provide us with more in-depth, appropriate and worthwhile answers.

Finally, if you need to change your goals for any reason, the act of writing them out will help you to have clearer vision regarding your changed circumstances. You will be better able to see why you need to change your goal, or conversely the pitfalls that are preventing you from reaching it. Sometimes the goal itself is not the problem; it is rather that we are following tangents, or meeting pitfalls along the way. We may not be functioning in the best and most efficient way to reach this particular goal. If in doubt, we should ask ourselves, 'Is it the goal which is not right? Or is it my method of trying to achieve it which is wrong?'

These questions are very difficult to answer unless we are writing out goals on a regular basis so that we can adjust and alter course (and methods) as necessary; or have confirmed for us that we are firmly on the right path.

So make the commitment and schedule goal-time in your diary now.

(Parts of this discussion are taken from my book You Can Do It! *(Reed Books).)*

BRAINSTORMING

Brainstorming is a very good way to solve problems, find direction and achieve goals. It is also a very powerful tool in helping to get a team motivated and in keeping motivation high. There is a lot of collective energy generated where even three or four like-minded people get together to discuss issues in common. If Gerry had regular brainstorming sessions with his team, he would find that motivation would certainly increase and that people would probably become enthusiastic about trying to reach team objectives.

To be effective, brainstorming should be carried out in a well-structured way. Three to seven people is an ideal number for this type of exercise. The number one rule is that anything and everything goes, and nobody is allowed to say anything negative or critical. It is important for the team that free-flowing and spontaneous communication can take place. People should be able to come out with the most ridiculous suggestions and fire out ideas without fear of censure or criticism. If there is an accepting, positive and free environment, then out of a myriad of useless solutions and ideas some gems will emerge. So anybody can say anything relating to the desired objective regardless of how far-fetched or impractical it may be, and it will be accepted in a positive way by the group. Doing this opens the channels to the subconscious mind, and provides a fertile ground for inspired thinking. The right climate is all-important if brainstorming is to work effectively.

One person should act as a scribe and note down all the ideas that emerge during the free-flow brainstorming session.

There should be a meeting a few days after the brainstorming session, in which a smaller group of people analyses what has been said and assesses the suggestions, ideas, and solutions which flowed freely in the initial session. From this they can pick what is of value, what is likely to work. This should be done in a positive climate and nothing of a critical nature should be relayed back to those who took part in the original brainstorming session. Usually somewhere between one in four and one in eight ideas or solutions will prove workable, and of value. It is from brainstorming sessions like this that great ideas are born and solutions to problems emerge.

If Gerry holds regular brainstorming sessions, in addition to using the other motivational tools to help inspire and enthuse his team, he will undoubtedly increase motivation and end up with a team who work well together, feel valued and have a sense of common purpose.

Gerry must be the innovator, lead the way, and quite deliberately set out to help motivate and inspire team members through the methods given. This way he will get his team up and running — and also winning.

SOME TANGIBLE WAYS OF REWARDING PEOPLE

Motivation, as we have seen, must come from within, but can be inspired from without. Rewarding people in tangible ways can be a help in increasing self-motivation. Reward systems have their place and are an appreciation for loyalty, commitment and effort. Gerry could implement some of the following suggestions to reward his team:

- Give extra time off.
- Take the team out for a good meal on a regular basis (firm pays, of course).
- Publicly thank them for their performance.
- Shout the team and their partners an occasional fun night out.
- Set up a bonus incentive scheme.
- Award a small extra salary increase right across the board for goals achieved.
- Ask each team member in turn to conduct a training session or demonstration.
- Give other material rewards as appropriate for objectives achieved

(e.g. a set of outdoor furniture, a good quality briefcase, etc.).
- Have fun competitions, with prizes like a fun night out or a weekend away for two.

Michael Le Boeuf, in his excellent book *How to Motivate People,* recommends (p. 103):

1. Reward solid solutions to ensure the achievement of long-range goals.
2. Reward risk-taking, applied creativity, and decisive action to boost the spirit of entrepreneurship.
3. Reward smart work, simplification, quietly effective behaviour and quality work to improve productivity.
4. Reward loyalty and working together to foster team-work and co-operation.

He also advises the following strategies:

Reward	*Instead of*
1. Solid solutions	1. Quick fixes
2. Risk-taking	2. Risk-avoiding
3. Applied creativity	3. Mindless conformity
4. Decisive action	4. Paralysis by analysis
5. Smart work	5. Busy work
6. Simplification	6. Needless complication
7. Quietly effective behaviour	7. Squeaking joints
8. Quality work	8. Fast work
9. Loyalty	9. Turnover
10. Working together	10. Working against

If Gerry followed the above principles, plus the other guidelines given in this chapter, he would certainly be moving the right way to have a highly motivated team!

EXERCISES

1. Do you know your company's vision, and do you have a vision for the part you wish your team to play in achieving this?

2. Do you communicate your vision to your team?

3. Do you call regular team meetings?

4. Do you hold brainstorming sessions?

5. Do you set inspiring, realistic and achievable goals for your team? Do you break them into workable stepping-stone goals?

6. Do you motivate and support individual members of the team by giving them one-to-one supervision on a regular basis?

7. Are you a strong and decisive leader whose competency, strength and decisiveness your team can rely on and from whom they can draw the strength and calmness they need to cope with the pressure?

8. Overall, how well do you think you measure up to the demands of leadership, as outlined in this chapter?

TO SUM UP

Managers manage.
Coaches coach.
Team leaders manage, coach and — above all — lead.
The buck stops with you.

CHAPTER FOURTEEN

Team building

Steven was the art director of a large international advertising agency. As such, he was responsible for fourteen people, all very much individualists.

One of Steven's major tasks in the fiercely competitive advertising world was to keep his team motivated to perform to a very high level. To do so it was essential that they function as a closely knit and innovative unit. Steven had a happy knack of keeping this team of highly creative people switched on and enthusiastic. As a result the working environment was stimulating and challenging, but also very supportive. With few exceptions, his staff related well to each other and to him, and though they did not always agree on everything, they were a cohesive and loyal working team which usually achieved above average results.

In his running of his unit Steven considered one thing very important — he believed in allowing them considerable flexibility and freedom of functioning. He did not care how they achieved results as long as they *did* achieve results (for instance one team member chose to work outdoors and did so whenever possible). In allowing them to function in a way which was right for their individual personality and working style, Steven was very wise, because ultimately we can only perform at top level if we are allowed to truly be ourselves. Steven found that flexibility of functioning paid off time and again in outstanding performance and ongoing commitment to achieving top results.

In case Steven is beginning to sound like a paragon as a leader, let me assure you he isn't. Certainly he has learnt a great deal about how to lead through gradually acquiring the skills to do so, but above all it has been through a process of trial and error. Fortunately one of

Steven's strengths is that he has had the ability to learn from his mistakes.

When he first assumed his present position as head of the art department, Steven wanted to run a tight, efficient ship; consequently he overstructured his running of the department, and expected people to conform to his rather 'old hat' way of managing, losing a couple of extremely talented innovators and creative thinkers in the process. For instance, he insisted that one man be at his drawing board by 8.30 in the morning. The artist concerned was not a 'morning' person and did not hit his optimum functioning time until afternoon, but he was often still doing really creative work until late in the evening. This particular team member used to irritate Steven because he appeared to sit around half-asleep all morning. Steven and he became very frustrated with each other, until eventually this quite brilliant artist left to go to an agency where he could work flexible hours.

On another occasion, Steven had insisted that a young artist, who was full of promise, work in the office instead of allowing her to work half the day at home as she had requested. Along with her sister, she shared the responsibility of caring for an elderly parent. Zoe always met the deadlines imposed upon her by job requirements, but Steven nevertheless insisted that she work normal office hours. Consequently he also lost her to an agency who didn't care where or when she worked, as long as she delivered the goods. Within a short period of time Steven realised that he had lost one of the most promising juniors he had ever seen and was unable to find anyone of her calibre to replace her.

Having learnt from these experiences, Steven acknowledged the value of allowing people to work in the setting that best suited them, and during the hours they preferred. This way they were mentally at their best, and had a high energy flow.

SUCCESSFULLY MOTIVATING THE TEAM

The leader of tomorrow will have to nurture the talented and innovative people who work for them. He or she will need to recognise that the way to really get the best results from people and motivate them to achieve will be to tap into their *natural* workflow;

the way in which they learn, process, think, act and perform the best. To do anything else will result in second-grade results. Flexibility, and understanding what motivates the person to work best, is what it is all about. It takes confidence and wisdom to lead in this way, but ultimately it is the only way which will lead to top-level functioning and best results. The days of putting the accent on structure and conformity have long since gone, and the leader or manager who tries to impose this on people will be left far behind; their style of leadership will be as out-of-date and ineffectual as the now obsolete 'autocratic' style of managership.

For one thing, people all have a different mode by which they communicate, take in and process information. It is to do with the way our brain functions. To try to force people to work, learn and perform in a way which is foreign to them is as ineffective as trying to fit a square peg into a round hole. Since Steven learnt this lesson, the members of his team have shown outstanding results in their work, both on an individual and team basis.

Flexible people survive disasters and overcome problems because they have learnt to think laterally and are willing to explore alternative options. They 'roll with life's punches' and keep on going. They also learn to work and perform in the way which is right for them and to allow others to do the same. Inflexible people cannot adapt in a positive way to change, are often highly stressed, and therefore less likely to stay the course and succeed. Unfortunately they also tend to extend their rigid attitude to others — to the detriment of the latter. They often fall into depression and may experience despair.

Steven took his role as team leader very seriously. He believed in structuring the team and building people up in such a way that they performed well both on an individual and on a team basis. He identified the strengths and weaknesses within the team (and within the individual) and set goals to keep both team and personal motivation high. He also regularly assessed team needs. In this he was very wise because assessing performance provides appropriate and flexible structure — not only for the team, but for the individual. To facilitate this he met regularly with individuals, and got the team together for discussion and also, when necessary, for performance reviews.

As team leader, Steven recognised that he must walk a fine line between friendliness and self-disclosure on the one hand and remaining objective on the other. There has to be a balance between mateship and maintaining discipline. The buck stops with the manager or team leader, and Steven never forgot that. He had the required emotional maturity and good judgement to know when to be relaxed, open and warm to team members, and when to put on the leader's hat, set limits, and accept final responsibility. He also knew when to give constructive criticism. His good judgement and experience had taught him to 'get the balance right'. The positive results he achieved from the team reflected this.

Steven learned to recognise that different people respond to different methods of communication. One person will respond to warmth, a certain amount of intimacy and a lot of encouragement. Another (through their own inadequacies and past injuries) will respond only to quiet firmness and a show of strength. Yet another gets bored if not continually challenged and stimulated to the point where they are forced to extend still further. As a good leader, Steven knew how to press the right buttons in people to get the best results.

Getting to know one's people is the key. If there are too many people to get to know, then teams need to be split up into sub-teams. Restructuring in this way within organisations is often long overdue.

Steven believed in the value of good communication, and sought to establish this, both within the team as a whole and also with each individual. During a fifteen-minute team meeting each morning he would discuss the day's work, anticipate and ask for practical solutions to the problems which might arise that day, ask for input from anybody who wanted to discuss their work, give support and encouragement (and encourage others to do the same) to any member who was experiencing difficulties. People often emerged from the meeting on a bit of a high, or at least with a positive attitude towards their work. In addition he would take the opportunity throughout the day to interact with as many members of the team as possible, and encouraged them to interact in a supportive and positive way with each other.

At least twice a week Steven called a longer team meeting at which he gave various members the opportunity to chair the meeting. At this meeting he would motivate his team by setting goals for them to achieve as a team, reviewing overall team performance and asking for suggestions as to how they, as a cohesive working unit, could achieve even better results. He would look at problems and brainstorm for solutions, give people the opportunity of raising problems and others the opportunity of responding to them with ideas and positive solutions (often thoughts based on their own past experience). He also actively encouraged members of the team to use these meetings as a time to bring up difficulties and problems they were personally experiencing in their work. Steven made it very obvious that he regarded it as a show of strength to have the honesty to ask both for ideas and for support. Often these sessions were held at a time when the team as a whole could review and reassess their goals, and measure how their performance was standing up. They frequently brainstormed as to how they could perform and extend themselves even further to achieve longer-term team goals, and regularly assessed their progress.

Through these, Steven kept motivation high and built a highly successful and hard-working team.

SOME COMMENTS ON STEVEN'S LEADERSHIP

This is the best agency I have ever worked for. They're a great bunch of people in our team. We have a lot of fun and there's a really good atmosphere. We're always sending each other up in a humorous way, but if there are any problems everybody immediately closes ranks and clusters around to help the person out, or find a solution. Of course it comes from Steven — we all know that, and he's just about the best team leader and head of department I have ever had. I've always said that if you want to have a good working environment and a team that really pulls together and is highly motivated, then it's got to start from the top. And that is exactly what we are seeing happening here.

What I also like about working for this agency, and Steven in particular, is that they encourage you to further your own knowledge. If this means that they have to pay for or subsidise you to do additional courses to become more expert in your job, then they will do so. Steven frequently asks who needs to do what in the training line, to help them perform better. We are asked to think about our needs in this area, and a couple of times a year most of us are sent on some course or another. Not only work-related courses either, but courses which will help us to further our own personal growth such as Confidence Building or Communication or whatever.

I think this says it all about an organisation's interest in you as a person, that they will fund you to do courses which help you on a personal level. If they're willing to invest in you as a person to that extent, it reflects their attitude towards you in the workforce. It says a lot really about how they value their people. Yes, I think Steven is so much more than just a manager or head of a department. He is a real leader. (One of Steven's team members.)

I believe that we have one of the best creative teams in the industry in Steven's department, and I think it's largely due to his leadership. I know from having come up through the ranks in advertising myself that it's not always easy to get through to all the creative people, because where you get brilliance you often get a volatile temperament. And when you get an innovator you often get a nonconformist.

We've got managers and we've got leaders in this organisation and there is a big difference between the two. The manager manages people but the leader really leads, and sets an example. Here are some of the reasons why I believe Steven is such a good leader.

He is not afraid to delegate. He doesn't try and make himself indispensable and do the lot himself. He builds people's confidence by delegating. Also he has his priorities right. Priority work is given priority, and he doesn't fluff around and indulge in a lot of 'pie-in-the-sky' thinking, which a lot of people in this line of work tend to do. Because of this he encourages his team to do the same.

He's not afraid to admit when he's made a mistake, to ask for advice or seek other opinions. When uncertain he'll re-evaluate the situation and take time to think things through, again setting an excellent example to his team.

Of course he operates by an open-door policy, and would not have the highly motivated team he does if he failed to do so. But nevertheless he schedules personal time to complete tasks which demand concentration. He lets it be known that for a period of time each day he is unavailable to people, except in an emergency.

Though the guy is supportive, he doesn't become embroiled in other people's problems and crises. He will explore the options with them but has the ability to stand back and leave the decision and the implementing of that decision to them. This above all, I believe, makes him an above average leader.

There is a quite outstanding atmosphere in his department. For one thing, there is enormous trust between team members, and between Steven and the team. They obviously have good motives towards each other. Yes, I think the atmosphere of trust is what makes it work. (The head of the advertising agency.)

THE SUCCESSFUL TEAM LEADER

There are a number of personal qualities which successful team leaders show in common. First, they are aware of the importance of good working relationships and of the need for team members to interact with each other on all levels, and they provide ample opportunities for this.

Good team leaders know, and are committed to, the aims of their organisation. This sets the standard for others, who, in discussions of goals and mission statements at their team meetings, will take their cue from their leader.

Being able to relate in a comfortable and positive way with all the members of the team, a good leader can quietly assume the leadership role in a non-threatening way. This gives the team the security they need to get on with their job. A reliable anchorperson (the leader) always reduces stress in the working environment because of the secure base they provide for others.

The effective leader also demonstrates an openness to receive suggestions and criticism, and welcomes ideas from others if they prove to be better than their own. Inwardly secure, they can encourage input from team members.

An inspiring leader models an openness and willingness to keep learning, and actively seeks ongoing training in his or her own work, paving the way for others to do the same.

Another way in which a leader may model desirable behaviour to the team is by refusing to indulge in gossip, listen to the same or put others down. In this way a positive, honest environment is created in which healthy communication is emphasised. The leader who cares for the team does not betray confidences or pass on information which might have a negative effect on others. In other words the right focus is maintained to achieve results.

Team spirit is fostered by this positive climate, aided by constant encouragement. An effective leader will give support to both the individual and the team generally, but will not act impulsively by rushing in to fix things or rescue somebody if things appear to be going wrong. Rather he or she will stand back and objectively assess what should be done. Then through discussion, the team member can be encouraged to fix the problems themselves, coming up with their own solutions.

Another way in which a good team leader can set a good example is by pacing himself or herself, and endeavouring to achieve balance in both personal and work life. An eye can also be kept on those team members who appear to be failing to pace themselves. It is this sort of care for individuals in the team which distinguishes a good leader.

POSITIVE TEAM INTERACTION

It is essential, if a team is to maintain its impetus and high motivation, that there be good group interaction. In order to ensure this, clear, concise communication must be a priority. This is necessary so that objectives are achieved and misunderstandings prevented. It is also necessary so that the focus of the team is the same, and the overall thrust directed towards achieving the same objective. Otherwise the team as a whole will be robbed of its effectiveness.

Good relationships and team goodwill must be a priority; this is obvious. Hostility (veiled or otherwise) undermines team spirit and weakens the group's dynamics. Misunderstandings, jealousy, lack of tolerance for individual ways of functioning, etc., need to be sorted out early in the piece so that the team works in a constructive way, and the pathway is cleared for full co-operation. Only then will the dynamics of the team be positive, and its members be able to perform well as a group. Sometimes honest, open discussion is necessary to clear the air and remove blocks which may prevent this from happening. Nothing undermines a team as much as nebulous undercurrents which are allowed to develop and remain undealt with.

It is the responsibility of the team leader to bring these and other contentious issues out in the open so that they may be addressed and resolved. These things do not usually resolve themselves (as many people in a leadership capacity hope), and ignoring rather than defusing them has the effect of increasing their power. Painful though it may be, there is only one way to deal with the situation and that is to honestly confront the negative issues which are preventing members of the group from interacting in a healthy and constructive way.

RESOLVE CONFLICT EARLIER RATHER THAN LATER

The earlier conflict is resolved the better. People need to be given the opportunity to resolve conflict and causes of dissatisfaction as soon as possible. They also need to have the opportunity to express their doubts about what is happening, and about the roles they are expected to play. Expressing feelings defuses them; feelings which are left to build up will cause attitudinal and behavioural problems at a later stage. Unexpressed dissatisfaction and negative emotions can also cause passive resistance; as a result an insidious blocking of what needs to be achieved can occur. All blocks towards a willingness to co-operate towards achieving the same objectives and goals must be addressed as soon as they become apparent. It goes without stating that they must, of course, be addressed in a positive way. If they are not, then negative games — blaming, shaming, office politics, playing favourites, subtle undermining of the individual, etc. — begin to rear their ugly head. When this happens the team as a whole suffers and is undermined. It is essential to have a strong leader who will quickly confront the issues which need dealing with.

DIFFERENT STYLES THE TEAM LEADER MAY ENCOUNTER

It can be a useful exercise to look at the various styles sometimes found in members of the group. For the purposes of clarity we shall put them under the following headings while we examine them.

The observer:
- is hooked on process;
- reflects back to other people;

- reviews and observes;
- is aware of the facts;
- analyses.

The judge:
- is rational and logical;
- seeks balance;
- looks for honesty;
- evaluates and listens in-depth;
- deals in facts.

The questioner:
- challenges the accepted;
- challenges what is regarded as normal;
- is controversial;
- avoids the status quo and adopts the unconventional;
- stimulates and extends others' thinking;
- comes up with the unexpected.

The task controller:
- puts the emphasis on tasks not people;
- is concerned with details;
- is preoccupied with quality and performance;
- is constantly checking up;
- emphasises the objective to be achieved;
- is totally goal-oriented.

The conservative:
- avoids confrontation and challenges;
- glues the team together;
- is co-operative and builds relationships;
- tries to fill the gaps when necessary;
- is friendly and people-oriented;
- doesn't like taking risks, or doing things differently.

The innovator:
- comes up with bright ideas;
- motivates people;

- is inspiring and enthusiastic;
- is imaginative;
- tries the new and untried;
- is ingenious and has vision;
- has ideas which become strategies;
- can take others' ideas and build on them.

The abrasive member:
- challenges and confronts;
- is almost totally task-oriented;
- pushes people hard;
- can be intolerant as a driver;
- regularly analyses progress and institutes checks;
- is motivated by results.

The diplomat:
- is people-oriented;
- puts the emphasis on building relationships;
- enlists co-operation;
- wins loyalty and support for self and team;
- negotiates constructively;
- smooths oil on troubled waters;
- is warm and extroverted;
- tactfully influences others;
- sells ideas: the team — the product — the goal;
- creates harmony;
- extends bridges.

The team supporter:
- encourages;
- resolves conflict;
- is very supportive;
- is an excellent listener;
- makes people feel comfortable;
- creates a safe climate;
- gives advice;
- cares about people.

The professional:

- gives expert advice;
- objectively assesses situations/results/team needs/methods etc.;
- draws others out and finds their area of expertise;
- is thoroughly professional;
- is quietly confident;
- commands attention.

The team leader may have to deal with all of these different styles, and more, within the team itself. If this is the case they may have a difficult task. It is desirable that they themselves have many of the positive qualities to be found in these different modes of functioning.

The team leader's role, as Steven found, is to build people up so that they perform well on both an individual and team basis, to find out their areas of strength and weakness, and to help them to capitalise and build on the former, while gradually overcoming the latter. They need to structure the team to become a cohesive and co-operative working unit. By setting goals and realistic objectives which are achievable, they extend both the individual and the team. In meeting these, the team leader not only sets objectives and monitors performance but is sensitive to, and aware of, team needs as a whole.

Steven learnt very early in the piece that he had to provide a certain structure for his team members, but due to their extreme creativity, innovativeness and individuality, it had to be a very flexible structure (in fact minimal structure). The leader should both grow with the team and learn from the team, becoming more and more aware of what makes this particular team work well and 'turns them on'; for this keen powers of observation and insight are necessary. Different teams have different needs, and demand different forms of motivation. The wise leader learns the necessary keys.

SOME ESSENTIAL DOS AND DON'TS OF A GOOD TEAM LEADER

When Steven was asked to give some help to a new head of department within the agency, he listed the following dos and don'ts for a good team leader. They should:

- be able to relate well and comfortably with all members of the team;
- see themselves as a part of the team, and be involved in team effort;
- demonstrate an openness in considering other points of view, and acknowledge that others may have better ideas;
- actively seek ongoing education;
- be enthusiastic about having meetings to motivate the team, and deal with issues which arise; also keep enthusiasm high;
- share the vision of the organisation and pass it on to team members, and have regular measurement procedures in place;
- make sure that goals are clearly defined; also ensure that team members know and understand them;
- be willing to listen to and get alongside individual team members in a positive way, and encourage them to do the same with each other;
- be prepared to confront in a positive way when appropriate and necessary;
- if things are going wrong within the team, bring it out in the open and deal with it as soon as possible;
- be capable of pouring oil on troubled waters when necessary, but always be objective;
- be the anchorperson, and be prepared to take responsibility when necessary (it's what you're paid more for);
- analyse the needs of the team collectively and individually;
- learn how to best meet these needs;
- develop superb listening skills;
- find the incentives which motivate the individuals within the team — and the team itself.

The new head of department found Steven's advice and guidelines invaluable, and used Steven as her mentor for the first two years after taking up her new position.

THE VALUE OF HAVING A MENTOR

It can be extremely valuable to have a mentor who is prepared to share their experience and know-how, and who will also take the new leader or manager under their wing. If we can observe and study at first hand the pointers which make a leader effective, we are far less likely to make a lot of unnecessary mistakes. Admittedly we also learn from our mistakes, but sometimes a mentor who has trodden the path before us can point out unnecessary pitfalls. Also through a process of observing and communicating we can discover what makes a particular person so successful in their field. Obviously we would not have chosen this person unless they had outstanding qualities which we wish to emulate. If they are successful, and are achieving the desired results, then it makes sense to study their style and find out what they are doing right.

EXERCISES

1. What are the essential differences between a team leader and a manager?

2. Why was Steven such a good team leader? List the pertinent points as you see them.

3. What special qualities does a team leader need if they are to be effective as we move towards a new era in business?

4. Why do you feel some leaders/managers still over-control and remain inflexible?

5. When you compare your style of leadership with Steven's what differences are there?

6. Using Steven as a measuring stick, what changes do you need to make to upgrade, update and improve your own style of leadership?

7. What do you consider to be the most important point in keeping team motivation high?

8. What is the most significant thing you have learnt from this chapter?

9. All managers are not leaders, but all leaders have also learnt to manage well. Do you agree with this statement? Justify your answer.

TO SUM UP

Most people can learn to be good managers once they have acquired a set of techniques which work, but it takes special qualities, much thought, sensitivity and insight along with a broad range of skills, to be a leader.

CHAPTER FIFTEEN

Vision, goal setting and team motivation

Dean was the sales manager for a large international pharmaceutical company. As such his responsibility was to ensure that his products led the field in the medical market.

Dean was well aware of the difficulties his salespeople faced in trying to influence the medical profession (their major clients) to use their drugs. Competition was very fierce indeed, with other major drug companies trying, with all sorts of purchasing incentives, to woo the medical profession to use their products.

Another problem frequently encountered by his sales team was the difficulty in actually getting appointments with these extremely busy practitioners. Dean knew from his own experience that sometimes a salesperson would have to go back again and again before they could actually see their client, and even then they were not usually given the time to make a proper sales presentation. Sometimes they had to deliver their message in as little as five minutes. Dean empathised with his team and was able to relate to their difficulties.

Though Dean had good communication with his group and had himself experienced many of their problems, he was nevertheless failing to inspire and help motivate them to perform better. In fact, at team meetings a lot of time was spent focusing on the difficulties of their job, rather than on constructive ways in which they could overcome these difficulties. What Dean should have been doing besides allowing people to air their problems was to focus in a positive way on the *advantages* of their job, and how they could help each other to *overcome* the very real problems they were encountering. Had he encouraged the team to focus more positively in this direction they would have undoubtedly been able to help each other and find answers.

It is a known fact that where a few positively thinking, right-minded people are gathered together to find solutions to problems, the answers will come. One person may not get the total answer, but they will perhaps get the beginnings of an idea which the next person will pick up on; then somebody else will carry it one step further. This is the way answers are found. Sometimes, quite out of the blue, one member of the group will make an inspired statement which provides the breakthrough the group is looking for. But this can only happen when the focus is positive, and it is the team leader's responsibility to ensure that it is. When a team operates in this way everybody feels supported.

Another thing Dean was failing to do was to set goals for his team as a whole, as well as for the individuals within the team. It is extremely difficult to keep a team motivated without the aid of goals to aim for. There is a great likelihood of the team becoming demotivated and losing direction if they are not constantly working to attain well-thought-out and pre-planned goals. These goals need to be of short, intermediate and long-term duration. Of course the latter should involve the setting of stepping-stone goals as this is a necessary process by which we can finally attain long term goals.

What Dean needed to do was to inject new life, enthusiasm and impetus into the group by encouraging them to work in a more structured way, working to pre-planned goals. These not only needed to be discussed and set, but also to be continually reviewed and written out. Furthermore Dean needed to take the lead in changing the climate from negative to positive. He should have been encouraging his team to see problems as obstacles to be overcome, and difficulties as growth steps to their further development in gaining confidence and expertise.

There are always new solutions to old problems, just as there are always ways of overcoming difficulties. When we are fully extending ourselves because of difficulties which may challenge us, we are forced to develop skills and inner resources which we may otherwise not have done. Change and a new direction must come from Dean now, and perhaps the best way for him to accomplish this is to be honest and tell his team that a negative climate has been allowed to take over, but from now on things are going to be different — and *he* is prepared to start the ball rolling. If he asks for their co-operation he may be surprised at the support and willingness he receives. It often takes only one determinedly positive-thinking person to initiate things. The very fact that Dean puts before his team the new goal-setting plan, and involves them in it, will in itself begin to activate enthusiasm and a necessary change of environment.

SOME COMMENTS FROM DEAN'S COMPANY

When I first started this job I was filled with enthusiasm and drive. I was going to get out there and 'make a killing' to use the department jargon. However, gradually I feel I have lost momentum. A part of the reason for this is that over an eight-year period things have become so much tougher; it's a much more fiercely competitive market place now, and you have to work nearly three times as hard to even maintain ground. So after a time I guess all this began to affect me, and while I still seem to be putting in as much time and energy, somehow I've lost enthusiasm and felt as if I was losing direction too.

However, I think change is beginning to occur and it's coming from Dean, actually. Just a few days ago he called a team meeting and told us that we had all slipped into a rut and he largely blamed himself for that. He said he had been neglecting to lead the way with a positive attitude, and had also failed to set the goals for us to aspire to. He outlined goal plans we were going to work towards and asked for our co-operation in setting the goals we needed as a team, inviting our input. I really appreciated this as I've had some ideas about these things in the past, but have never really had the opportunity to air them. He told us that, in addition, he was going to be working more closely with each one of us to set goals we could keep working towards. After listening to him I really experienced new hope. He's got my support anyway. What sold it for me really was when he took responsibility and said that he had been slack in not seeing the need before. (One of the sales team.)

I did not quite know what to do about the problems with our sales team because I was aware that Dean was very supportive of his team and was doing his best to help them. This particular group just seemed to be lagging and seemed to have lost their incentive, although they had no real complaints and couldn't particularly put their finger on why.

I did some thinking about the problem, and then had a talk with Dean. When we analysed the problem as a whole we realised that some outside expert advice might be needed, because it was obvious Dean was doing the best he could, and didn't know what else he should be doing. There was a missing key somewhere. So what we came up with was the idea of seeking the advice of a professional. He worked privately with Dean for a little while, giving him pointers as to what he could do to turn the team around. The plan is that Dean is going to implement these suggestions, give it three months, and see what changes occur in that time. If he doesn't then notice a difference, and find people becoming more enthusiastic and motivated, he will put the whole team through a series of seminars geared towards teaching them how to set and achieve goals, and how to keep their motivation high. He will, of course, go through these sessions himself with them.

I like the fact that Dean is so willing to seek advice and to implement what he has been told to do. I think we're on the right path, and I'm just sitting back quietly and waiting to see the results. I have a gut feeling that we are going to get there. (Dean's managing director.)

VISION PRECEDES THE SETTING OF GOALS

First we need to have vision, and once we know what that vision is, we then set goals to implement it.

If we are to be a catalyst for motivation we need to share our vision with the team. To set goals without vision is almost to work blind, for it is vision which gives the impetus and desire to set the goals in the first place. It is also vision which motivates people to attain agreed upon goals. (See also chapter fourteen.)

SHARE YOUR VISION

I have found that too few leaders realise the importance of sharing their vision, and in particular the vision of the company as a whole.

Consequently the opportunity to inspire people to a high degree of commitment and motivation in setting and achieving company goals is lost. Without the drive and impetus of vision, goals lose their power and excitement. Excitement, enthusiasm and feeling are what really inspire and sweep people along to achieve the desired end result. Vision has been described as a magnet which draws the person or the team steadily towards the fulfilment of the goal. A person with vision has a driving force which will motivate them to reach and achieve their goal. Without it, it is hard for them to do so.

MEASURE YOUR PROGRESS

The achieving of goals is also a useful measure of performance. Without a regular setting of goals and measuring of such, a team or person can very easily lose direction, drifting along day by day doing what seems to be important at the time, or what comes up next. They also will be deprived of an important way of measuring both progress and performance.

Some questions which it is useful to ask the team would be the following:

- What is the overall vision for our company?
- What does our company as a whole wish to, and need to, achieve to fulfil it?
- What is our overall goal?
- What direction do we need to take to achieve this goal?
- Have we already started taking this direction?
- Do we need to change direction now to achieve our goals?
- What planning should we do now and in the future to achieve our goals?
- What part do we as a department/team play in achieving these goals?
- What team/department/organisational goals should we set at this time?
- What will aid us in achieving these goals?
- What is preventing us from achieving them?
- What can we do about it?
- How can we motivate ourselves (as a team and on an individual

basis) to ensure that we meet the target goals we set?
- How can we pull together as a team and support and motivate each other to do so?

KEEPING UP IMPETUS AND MOTIVATION

Confidence builds confidence — so set *achievable* goals, but ones which *extend* both the team and the individual. They must not be too difficult or too obscure or people will lose motivation and give up. Remember more ambitious goals can be set as progress is made and confidence increases. It is important to set stepping-stone goals to achieve major goals.

Have clearly defined goals, otherwise people will be in a state of inner conflict and confusion, which in turn robs them of direction, energy and commitment. Eliminate confusion and conflicting desires at the outset, because this demotivates people and leads to stress.

As can be seen, it is important to set goals that are achievable, and also to structure them so that they can be achievable. It is also important to show the team *how* goals can be achieved by the stepping-stone goal method (see Chapter 13).

In addition it is important that the team leader also works with the individual members of the group to encourage and aid them in the setting of personal goals (which are compatible with team goals). This helps the person to further their career path. The ideal time to do this is during regular one-to-one supervision sessions. When both team and individual goals are a priority and are being given the attention they deserve, it is unlikely that anyone will lose direction or motivation. There is no greater way of pulling the team together than to be regularly setting and jointly striving to achieve goals. It also reduces conflict, for the simple reason that it encourages everybody to focus in the same direction and aim for the same end.

The team leader who does not use goal-setting (with all that this entails) is failing to use a valuable tool to pull the team together, keep everybody working in the same direction, and keep motivation high. They are making their task in leading a team so much more difficult, and are also failing to use one of the best methods available to achieve significant and long-term results.

EXERCISES

1. Have you 'caught the vision' for your company?

2. Have you shared this vision with your team?

3. Do you regularly set goals for your team?

4. Do you involve them in this goal-setting process?

5. Do you set stepping-stone goals to ensure that a pathway is created to achieve major goals?

6. Do you have regular and measurable goal-checks?

7. Does the team as a whole discuss goals and check progress on a regular basis?

8. Do you work with the individual members of the group to set goals and help them achieve their personal work goals?

9. Have you found the setting of goals to be a good way of pulling the team together and keeping motivation high among its members?

10. Do you use this tool as fully as you should to extract the best from your team?

11. What about your own goals? How do they fit in with your company goals?

(These exercises also reinforce those in chapter thirteen)

TO SUM UP

Just as an individual who has no goals is likely to lose direction, like a rudderless small craft drifting around the harbour, so a team without the power of goals will, like a powerless large vessel, drift aimlessly at the whim of every wind and current.

(Parts of this chapter are taken from my book *You Can Do It!*)

CHAPTER SIXTEEN

Parent-adult-child ego states

Rowena, a manager at a medium-sized chemical manufacturing plant, was very good at her job and generally achieved a high level of efficiency. This was reflected in a smooth-running and well-organised department. She had a business management degree and was obviously going places. She had her sights on a senior management position, and had made up her mind that if she hadn't achieved this within the next three years where she was, she would move on. In the meantime she aimed to further her career by taking additional management study courses.

Rowena's department ran well and operated smoothly, and was noted for a consistently high level of productivity. However, there were some areas to do with relating to people in which she was having difficulty functioning adequately as a manager. Rowena had half a dozen people in her rather large department who were termed 'difficult to get along with'.

Every one of these people had, in their own way, caused her considerable problems. For a person who was reasonably self-controlled and who got along well with others, she was surprisingly thrown by them and reacted very negatively. One or two she suspected of being deliberately obstructive and difficult in order to see how far they could go. One challenged her to see at which point she would set her limits with them. Another frequently got her to the point where she felt on the verge of losing her temper. As she said to one of her colleagues, 'Dan can make me lose my temper faster than anybody else I know. I don't know what it is about him, but to me he's like a red rag to a bull. I know I'm not the only one he does it to — the others find him difficult to work with too. But in my position I should have better control and should not let him have this effect on me.' Her colleague's reply: 'Well you're only human after all and I don't know of anybody who can get along with him', didn't help much.

Another staff member would whine and act like a dependent child when Rowena asked her to do anything. This had the effect of making Rowena overreact to the woman, and come on a little too strongly. At this point the woman concerned would go to her workmates complaining that Rowena was picking on her again.

Rowena's own personal assistant was prone to manipulating Rowena to achieve her own ends. She would dodge unpleasant tasks or avoid accepting responsibility for anything which did not go well. For quite some time Rowena had believed her assistant (who was a very likeable person), and had only recently begun to realise what game was being played out. Sally always had such a good excuse why she was not able to control the situation or was not to blame.

But perhaps Rowena's most difficult trial was Joe, who had been with the plant since it opened and who thought he knew it all. At times he refused outright to take orders from her, and if she did lay down the law would argue with her, giving her a hard time. He was quite capable of being rude and aggressive, and again was one of the few people who could cause the normally emotionally stable Rowena to reach the point of losing control and yelling back at him.

This small handful of people were beginning to shake Rowena's confidence in her own ability to be a good manager, and, particularly when she was overtired or stressed, were causing her to act in ways she knew were inferior and which she did not really approve of. This was a pity because she coped very well with the rest of the staff. Thinking the situation through, Rowena realised that they were all playing devious games, and decided that she would not be hooked into playing along with them. However, even this knowledge did not help her sufficiently to counter the game-playing.

It was not until Rowena took a one-day course in transactional analysis (parent-adult-child ego states, or P.A.C.) that she felt she had found the key to correct the situation. Learning this skill was a tremendous boost to her confidence, and made her feel far more in control of the situation when people became difficult. Though it took time for her to apply the principles she had learnt, she nevertheless consistently tried to use them, and over a three-month period found that they were beginning to work.

Gradually Rowena came to feel more and more comfortable with her new skills, while her associates found they needed to adapt to her different way of handling difficult or confrontational situations. However, adapt they did — because we teach people how to treat us — and from then on things began to improve for Rowena. As she later said to a colleague, 'I don't care if they hate me, as long as they respect me, and finally I feel that these particular people may be beginning to do just that.'

Perhaps the most difficult aspect of learning and acquiring new skills is the temptation to fall back into our old habits or patterns before the new patterns of behaviour feel natural to us. Eventually, however, there is a point at which acquired learning becomes instinctive functioning — the point at which we feel that the skills we have acquired are just a natural extension of our behaviour. Rowena found that it was much easier to be in control when this process began to occur, and she no longer felt awkward using these tools. She had reached a breakthrough and started to achieve much better results.

At the same time she stopped castigating herself every time she blew it, and, for instance, allowed Sally to get away with something she didn't like. Instead she went back to the drawing board, replayed the scenario in her mind and analysed where she had gone wrong, and how she could handle the same situation in a better way in the future. As time progressed Rowena grew in confidence, and became far more skilled in handling difficult and obstructive people. For her it was a major hurdle which she felt she had overcome, and one that no longer held her back and undermined her otherwise very good managerial skills.

COMMENTS FROM ROWENA'S DEPARTMENT

I don't know what it is about Rowena, but she seems to have far more control now than she used to. She also seems to be much more confident in the way she handles things, and people. This is particularly important in this department because we have a few difficult people who will give her a rough ride if they can. They used to be able to really stir her up. At times I sensed that she was at the point of either bursting into tears or shouting at them. However over the last few months she seems to be far calmer and more able to keep her cool in difficult situations.

I guess you can expect that there'll always be some troublemakers in any work place, but it's very important, I believe, that you've got a manager who knows how to deal with them firmly. If they don't it makes the rest of us feel a bit insecure, and certainly puts us a bit on edge. The job's difficult enough as it is without having people like this play up and get away with it. (One of Rowena's staff.)

I have been suggesting Rowena do a course in transactional analysis for some time now, because I don't know how I personally would have coped in the position I hold without it. I have found it to be one of the most valuable skills I have ever learnt. I'm so glad that she finally saw the light and studied this particular method of interacting with people. Now that she has learnt these excellent people-management skills, I have every confidence that she will be able to cope much better with the difficulties she has been encountering.

I find that not only did learning parent–adult–child techniques give me an added advantage in interacting with people, but it built my confidence to a marked degree. It also gave me the means to exercise more inner control. I was able to make the changes I needed to, within myself — and above all perhaps to see that I needed to make certain changes in my own personal style. Now that I know that Rowena has learnt this skill I am confident that she will be able to cope better, because she has enormous potential. Full credit to her for recognising that she needed to further her skills in the people-management area. (Rowena's senior manager.)

HOW TRANSACTIONAL ANALYSIS (P.A.C.) WORKS

We all have within us three ego states: a *parent ego state*, of which there are two sides — the nurturing, supportive parent and the critical, authoritarian parent; an *adult ego state*; and a *child ego state*. The child ego state also has two aspects to it. One relates to our free child within, which is humorous, spontaneous and creative. This aspect also embraces the feeling side of our being, and indeed all feelings, whether negative or positive must evolve from our child ego state. The other aspect of our child ego state is not quite so pleasant: this is where we find the rebellious, defiant, wilful, and selfish child. The dependent state also comes from this more negative aspect of our child ego state.

I am giving only a very brief, condensed version of the ego states here, in the hope of encouraging people to read further about them. (See, for example, *I'm Okay – You're Okay* by Dr Harris.) However, even a quick overview can show how these ego states are a valuable tool in interacting with other people and can give us the opportunity to learn about our own functioning, providing some insight into why other people respond to us as they do. In no way can this be regarded as a complete study of transactional analysis. I would urge the reader to study this further, and if possible to attend one of the many courses available which will teach this skill more fully.

P.A.C. can be used in two ways. We can look inwardly to our own behaviour and understand how we operate (and make the necessary changes to our mode of operation). We can also use P.A.C. in our interactions with other people in order to achieve better communication with them, to defuse conflict when we see it arising, and to interact in a more positive way with other people. Knowledge of this skill gives us more control and a great deal more understanding both of ourselves and of our relationships with others.

THE CHARACTERISTICS OF THE EGO STATES

We need to understand at the outset that P.A.C. when referring to child, adult and parent does not relate to age or status. For instance we all have a *child* ego state regardless of our age, and will see the child in us come through until the day we die. A four-year-old pulling the legs off its teddy bear is acting in a *critical parent* state, while a two-year-old crooning to a doll is in a *nurturing, supportive parent* ego state. The *adult* deals only in facts and logic. When in this state we weigh up, assess, consider, rationalise, and make decisions. No feelings are involved with the adult ego state.

Once it is clearly understood that the ego states relate to the way we think (internalise) and also to the way we interact with other people on the external level, it is easier to understand their value and how they can be utilised.

MOVING FROM ONE EGO STATE TO ANOTHER

We are all the time in one of the ego states, both in our thinking and in the way we act, and we very rapidly jump from one to another: 'I feel lousy' (child) . . . 'I will go to bed and have a good rest' (nurturing, supportive parent) . . . 'I ought to finish my work first, though, and be prepared for tomorrow' (critical parent) . . . 'Blow, I'm sick of having to work harder than anybody else; it's not fair' (defiant child) . . . 'Let's think this through — if I go to bed early because I'm tired and leave my work till tomorrow morning I will cope with it much better; I'm not doing any more tonight' (adult).

As you will observe, the thought processes have jumped from one ego state to another within seconds, and I have ended up sorting out my confused thinking by finally analysing the problem with my adult and making a decision in that state. This is an example of how we are all the time internalising in one of the ego states, and also how the adult (being the wise decision-maker) can often sort out unresolved, confused thinking.

THE POWER OF THE ADULT EGO STATE

One of the adult ego state's greatest strengths lies in this ability to resolve confused thinking and sort out inner conflict; it does this by assessing the situation logically and then making a decision. As we grasp the fundamentals of P.A.C. we have much more control over our thinking, and can more deliberately change our thinking processes, for instance replacing the critical parent thought processes ('I must do it', 'I should get organised') with adult thinking ('I'm going to do this,' 'I choose to take this option'). The latter uses the more positive thought which comes from adult ego state thinking, instead of the more negative thought which comes from critical parent ego state thinking (I must, I ought, I should). This empowers us and gives us more control, both of ourselves and of the situation.

THE PULL FROM THE PAST

When we indulge in critical parent-type thinking, we usually invoke a negative feeling response in ourselves. This comes from our childhood. Even though we are adults, we still have locked-in negative feelings which result from unpleasant memories of childhood. Like a hotline to our emotional memory-bank this ego state connects us instantly to what happened in our childhood. The fact that we may not remember the event that evoked these unpleasant memories has nothing to do with our present emotional response as an adult.

Often other people will provoke an almost irrationally angry or negative emotional response from us and we may wonder why we are reacting so strongly. Our common sense may tell us that we are quite able to handle the situation in a calm and logical way, but it is almost as if our emotional response is at war with our logic; and in a sense it is. Emotion, of course, has nothing to do with logic. We may be able to handle things very well (and know we should be able to) on the level of logic, but still have a strong, negative or unsettling emotional reaction to a certain person or situation. Understanding is half the battle, and hopefully once we accept that emotional responses have little to do with logic, and that we are still responding to those voices and situations from the past, we will be far more in control of the situation. All we need do then is to acknowledge the feelings — and then move on and assume control with our adult.

USING THE ADULT STATE FOR SELF-TALK

Rowena on her transactional analysis course learnt to mentally self-talk along certain lines when 'stirred up' by some of the aggressive members of her staff. 'Okay, so Fred immediately makes me feel angry because of his aggressive attitude. I accept that he does. Nevertheless, despite this feeling, I choose not to feed it or to respond to it. I will handle Fred with assertiveness and strength, and will therefore keep my cool regardless of how badly he acts.'

When we understand that Fred is very good at hooking either our critical and over-controlling parent, or our defiant and rebellious child, making us want to shout back at him, we begin to handle the situation in a calmer and more positive way. Just knowing and understanding what Fred can do to us empowers us to deliberately *choose* to act in an adult way, and therefore to respond assertively, using our adult, because to be in the adult is to be assertive. Once

Rowena learnt that these half-dozen difficult staff members were 'hooking' her critical parent or her rebellious child she was able to assume far more control for herself, and therefore to handle things in a much more effective way.

KNOWLEDGE IS POWER — IN A GOOD SENSE

We, like Rowena, may first have to shift ego states in our head in order to gain inner control. We are then far more likely to handle the situation with confidence and wisdom. Rowena found that once she had moved into the right ego state mentally (*internally*) she was then able to be in the right ego state *externally* when dealing with these rather difficult people.

Very early in the piece Rowena learnt that remaining in her adult ego state was the way to get her point home and to maintain control. Though at times they made it difficult for her to do so by being aggressive, getting upset or pressuring her, she nevertheless was able to maintain control of herself (and of the situation) by remaining in her adult ego state. She would use adult terminology such as 'I understand your point, but as I have already explained, I am not going to change my mind on this for the reasons I have given you. Therefore any further discussion is a waste of your time and mine.' Remaining in her adult gave her confidence and the power to keep calm amidst considerable pressure. Once Rowena had studied, grasped and applied the concepts of P.A.C. she reported to her manager and colleagues that she didn't know how she had ever managed without it.

DEFUSING THE POTENTIALLY EXPLOSIVE SITUATION

Knowing and understanding the ego states and how they work is a particularly important asset for anybody in a charge position in industry, so effective is it in resolving conflict and in defusing potentially explosive situations.

When a person is being aggressive or is in their critical authoritarian parent, or rebellious, defiant child role (which resembles aggression anyway), the most effective way we can maintain control of the situation (and of ourselves), is to use our adult. When we do so we have a reasonably good chance of influencing the other person to go into their adult ego state. Just by maintaining control, refusing to be rattled, and speaking with logic and calmness, we can often influence the other to do the same — though it may take a few minutes before they calm down sufficiently to get into the adult ego state. It is undoubtedly our best shot at containing a negative or hostile situation.

WHEN TO USE THE NURTURING, SUPPORTIVE PARENT

The exception to getting straight into the adult ego state is when dealing with someone who is seriously upset. If their emotional reaction is more than what may be regarded as normal, it may be wise, initially, to get into our nurturing, supporting parent role for a short time. This is in order to draw their feelings out, and thereby 'defuse' the situation through other means.

The principle here is that if someone is extraordinarily upset they cannot and will not respond to logic, and are in no fit state to listen to anything we may have to say. Their own intense feelings act as a block which prevents them from even hearing the other person. All they want at this time is to be listened to, heard, and to know that their feelings are accepted (which doesn't mean accepting the rightness of their cause or necessarily agreeing with them). They are in no state, psychologically, to respond to anything other than good listening and sensitive 'drawing-out' skills. So the quickest way we can reach them (and thereby defuse the situation) is to act from our nurturing supportive parent, showing them we are willing to hear what they have to say. They also need to know that we accept that they are very upset.

At this time we might make statements like, 'You're very uptight aren't you?' or 'I can see that this has really upset you.' Usually there will then be a great rush of feelings released by the person. This can be unpleasant to take, but we need to realise that a feeling expressed is much safer than a feeling suppressed. If we are wise enough to draw them out gently for a few moments and accept the feelings (even though we are not necessarily accepting the facts), they will usually calm down a little.

I have found that usually within a short time I am able to get into my adult and start talking in adult terminology: 'Okay, so now that you have explained to me how you feel and I can see the effect this has had upon you, what do you think the solution is?' or 'I think I understand the strength of your feelings about this matter. Shall we sit down now and explore what your options are?' or 'This has been very upsetting for you, I can see that. Looking at it logically, what do you think needs to be done to resolve this?' At this point, providing feelings have been expressed and the person has lost some of the intense emotion and tension which accompanies these powerful negative feelings, they will now be ready to respond in an adult way to logical discussion.

YOU CAN USUALLY GO STRAIGHT INTO YOUR ADULT

It is not very often that the situation is such that you have to use your nurturing supportive parent first before getting into your adult state. Usually it is appropriate to move quickly into the adult ego state. There is also a good chance that you can defuse the situation by modelling adult behaviour. However, if not, it is even more important for you to maintain control. The trauma and stress will be less if *you* at least can do this, and that in itself is a personal victory.

The important thing, as Rowena found, is not to allow somebody else's critical parent to hook your defiant, rebellious child, and for you not to respond to their rebellious, defiant child by getting into your critical, authoritarian parent. This is how most upsets escalate. Too often we react to somebody in a negative ego state by responding in an equally inappropriate state. The critical, authoritarian parent and the defiant, rebellious child states are notorious for 'hooking' each other and therefore escalating conflict.

It takes a lot of self-discipline to remain in the appropriate ego state when one is becoming emotionally upset, but it is more important at this time to do so; two people out of control are unlikely to resolve anything in a positive way.

THE APPROPRIATE USE OF THE EGO STATES

The other ego states have their part to play as well. There is a time to be in our child and use humour to break tension, be playful and have fun with friends or crack a joke. There is also a time to be in our nurturing, supporting parent and offer to lend a hand if somebody is overloaded, look after somebody if they are ill, do that little bit extra if somebody is overtired, but I will not enlarge on these here, as I am primarily concerned with focusing on the issues which Rowena was encountering. However, I would urge you to do a proper study of this very useful skill yourself.

THERE IS ALSO A PLACE FOR THE CRITICAL PARENT EGO STATE

After what I have been saying, you may be surprised to learn that there is also a place for the critical, authoritarian parent ego state in our behaviour. In our working lives we are probably called to be in it approximately 10 percent of the time, according to our situation and position. And any parent will tell you that if they were not in this state occasionally their children would soon be out of control. Anyone in a position of authority in industry will agree that there are times when they have to set limits and take the final responsibility. Of course this is done after discussion with everybody involved, but eventually there does come the point where they need to have the strength to accept responsibility and make that final decision, sometimes at the risk of losing popularity. You cannot please all of the people all of the time.

When called upon to give (constructive) criticism we are also in our critical parent ego state, though of course we should ensure in this circumstance that we use adult terminology (see below).

THE THREE MINI EGO STATES WITHIN EACH OF THE MAJOR EGO STATES

Each of the major parent, adult, child ego states contains within itself its own breakdown of all of the other ego states, in a minor way. For example the parent also has within it a mini parent, adult and child. So when the person is having to assume the final authority in the previously described way, they should use adult terminology to do so, even though, strictly speaking, they are in their critical, authoritarian parent ego state. Though in the parent state they will be communicating in an adult way: 'I understand your position, but for the reasons I have already given you, I am unable to meet your request at this time. If the situation changes in the future then we can once more discuss things.'

As you can see, the authority person is having to set their limits by saying 'no', but they are doing so in a way (using adult terminology) which is, or should be, far more acceptable to the other. If they were to use critical, authoritarian parent language, even though strictly speaking they are in this state, it would be inappropriate for the situation, and they may invoke a rebellious, defiant child reaction in the other person.

To carry this one step further, if the authority person were to say, 'No, I can't allow you to do that, it's out of the question so it's not even an issue worth discussing,' they would not only be in the critical parent ego state (which may be appropriate if they are having to set limits), but would also be using critical parent ego state language, which is in most instances inappropriate. The former method is a much better way of handling a refusal and setting limits.

When Rowena recognised that she could set limits using her critical parent ego state without actually *sounding* as if she were dictating or controlling, it freed her up to handle situations better. It also gave her the confidence to handle them in a more confident and effective way. Her understanding of the mini ego states within the three major ego states proved extremely useful when dealing with some of the obstructive and difficult people she frequently had to interact with. She found, for example, that by staying in her adult with Sally, her assistant, she rendered the latter powerless to carry on manipulating her. Rowena was so helped by learning the skill of P.A.C. that she decided she would send her whole department on a course, and thereby get them all functioning at the same level in communicating with each other.

As for Rowena herself, she is going from strength to strength, and gradually achieving a breakthrough in her relationships with some of the people with whom she had hitherto experienced major problems. All of this has, of course, made her a far more confident and effective manager.

EXERCISES

1. Can you see the advantages of P.A.C. for you in your work situation?

2. What do you think is its most valuable aspect?

3. What changes would you expect to occur within the people with whom Rowena was having trouble, once she began to communicate with them according to the P.A.C. principles?

4. Can you think of times when you act from your critical parent state? your defiant child? your adult?

5. Can you see any advantages in using P.A.C. skills in your personal life?

TO SUM UP

Knowledge is power; it should make us more confident and highly skilled in the way we encounter every situation we are called upon to deal with.

CHAPTER SEVENTEEN

Prepare your people for change

Chris is the managing director of a wholesale distribution company. He has been recently appointed to this position after working as a senior accountant within the firm for a number of years. He has an extensive business background, and at a comparatively early age acquired degrees in accountancy and business management. Though an experienced businessman, Chris does not have a real understanding and grasp of how to manage people. He functions very much on the level of logic, and does not have much time for emotions; in fact when confronted with an honest display of feelings he tends to become embarrassed, and shy away. It is little wonder then that when it was necessary for his firm to relocate and to undertake major restructuring, he did not handle the situation at all well as far as his people were concerned.

Initially, when it became obvious that such major upheaval was necessary, Chris and his senior managers had several comprehensive discussions on the subject when they examined the most practical way to proceed and handle changes of this magnitude.

Unfortunately, however, very little time was spent discussing how the changes would affect their 230 workers. When one of the managers expressed concern about this issue Chris responded with 'Well, they'll just have to accept it and adjust to it. They may be unsettled for a while, but give them time and they will get used to it. Remember there are going to be some advantages for many of them because we will be redeploying them to different jobs. So some of them will carry more responsibility and will be in line for promotion. They will see it as a very positive career move.'

When the question was raised as to how much notice should be given to the staff of the impending changes, Chris was firmly in favour of not announcing them until the last minute, so not too much time would be wasted discussing and worrying about what was going to happen. The meeting was almost equally divided on the issue. Half of the managers agreed with Chris that the less people knew about the change, the less unsettled they would become. The other half had grave doubts that this was the best way to proceed, and felt that it was very risky to not give people adequate notice regarding changes of this magnitude. After some heated discussion Chris put the issue to the vote. The vote came out in favour of not informing people of the move until five weeks beforehand, and not discussing job restructuring until after the company had relocated. And so a mistake was made which was to cost this company nearly eighteen months of on-going problems.

There was a shocked reaction throughout the whole organisation when, five weeks before the impending move, news of it was announced by Chris at a meeting of all staff and management. People were upset, worried and confused. Some were upset at the thought of the move itself, but most were upset or angry because they had been given so little notice that it was happening. As one worker said, 'Shows how much they think of us — they didn't even have the decency to let us know early enough, so that we could adjust to the idea and make arrangements regarding travel if we needed to. This company can go jump in the lake as far as I'm concerned. From now on I'm going to look after number one.'

Within three months of having relocated their premises this distribution firm had lost approximately one-third of their key personnel. Many did not like having to travel further, or by different routes to work. Others were so angry that they had not been informed of the shift and of the different roles they were now expected to play, that they left as soon as they could obtain another job. Still more people could not adjust to the fact that they were expected to assume different responsibilities and learn new skills.

At first Chris and his senior managers tried to act as if nothing was wrong, but it was obvious that their assurance was forced. They shut their eyes to the negative climate in the vain hope that things would settle. Chris in particular seemed to be slightly amazed and rather bemused as to why people were taking so long to settle and to adjust to the new structure. 'I thought they would have adjusted by now, and realised that expanding their work skills is ultimately going to be to their own advantage,' was all he could say.

It took nine months of high stress before things began to settle. During this period the company suffered substantial losses in their regular client base, in good will and also financially. It was a hard lesson to learn, but in the end this managing director and his team admitted that they had made some major mistakes which had cost them dearly, and if given time again they would do things differently.

SOME COMMENTS FROM CHRIS'S COMPANY

I'm very disappointed in our senior management and especially in our managing director. They don't know the problems they have created for those of us at mid-management level. Thanks to their mishandling of this whole shift and the restructuring they have landed us with a lot of disgruntled, resentful personnel, and frankly I don't blame them for feeling this way. Even somebody who has never received any training in management policies would surely know that that is a disastrous thing to do. What were they thinking of, I ask you. You never give people more than one major change at a time to cope with and if you are going to bring about change surely you prepare them for it so they can adjust to the idea.

It's no wonder we've got the problems we have, and they might sit around shaking their heads and saying 'We didn't think it would turn out like this and what's wrong with everybody', but we, the managers, have got to try and keep things running smoothly and try to reassure and support these upset staff. I've got enough to do without being a combination of psychologist, nursemaid, and father confessor to these people. Now I'm finding the pressure of having to reassure and support these upset people, along with everything else, is just becoming too much. If things don't settle soon I will certainly be putting up my antennae to see what else is available in the market place. Who needs this? I certainly don't. The annoying part is that it could all have been avoided if only management had had the sense to handle the change in a better way. (One of Chris's managers.)

In some ways, of course, things are better since the move. For example we're working in better premises, we've got a nicer cafeteria, there is more room, and the building is more modern. However, that doesn't make up for the negative atmosphere and the unhappy spirit around the place. Everyone resents the fact that we were only given five weeks' notice of the shift.

People have been put into new jobs they don't want to do and into positions they can't really handle. It seems that most of us have had our jobs changed or restructured and we haven't even been asked how we feel about it, or if we want this to happen. That's the part that brasses me off. It's all just taken for granted that you'll grind on regardless what you think or how you feel. The powers that be can make these great earth-shattering decisions at the drop of a hat without considering you at all. (A member of staff.)

CHANGE AND ITS EFFECTS UPON PEOPLE

Change always brings its own particular stress — even an apparently beneficial change. We expect to experience stress when change occurs which is not to our liking, but it can be surprising when we encounter stress as a result of positive changes such as getting married, being promoted in one's job, the birth of a child, or moving to a better neighbourhood. Sometimes, when events such as these occur, people can really be upset and confused by the stress reaction to an event to which they have been looking forward.

This was one of the reasons why Chris made such a serious mistake. Because *he* was looking forward to the company's change of venue and was also looking forward to restructuring the company internally, he failed to recognise that both these major changes would cause stress even while bringing benefits to some.

In order to explain this phenomenon we have to understand that we function on two very different levels — the level of logic and the level of emotion, and that while logically we may accept our changed situation, emotionally we may experience inner confusion regarding it.

LOGICAL vs EMOTIONAL REACTIONS TO CHANGE

A man is promoted at work. He sees the promotion as being extremely good for his career and future prospects — he has worked for it, he is looking forward to it, and now finally it has occurred. Logically he accepts it wholeheartedly and welcomes it. Emotionally, however, it is another story. He swings from delight and anticipation, to doubt and feelings of insecurity. In the morning his feeling may be, 'Great, this is just what I wanted. At last my work has been recognised and now my career path is all upwards.' That evening he may experience a totally different reaction on the emotional level, and have feelings such as, 'If they knew what I was really like they wouldn't have promoted me. I don't know if I can handle this. I am feeling pretty insecure about my new role; I doubt that I'm up to it.'

This swinging of his emotional pendulum is perfectly natural and normal, and is in fact to be expected. However, if he doesn't expect that he will have wide emotional swings in the early stage of change, the experience can be disturbing. This particular man asked me, 'Am I going nuts or what? I've been wanting this promotion for so long and am mentally prepared for it, yet now my feelings about it are jumping around like a yo-yo.' What our friend needs to do is to accept that he is functioning on these two different levels. He will swing from positive to negative feelings until he adjusts to the change: it always takes much longer to adjust emotionally than it does logically. However, we do reach a point of consolidation when we are able to accept and adjust with no further problems.

ALLOW TIME TO ADJUST TO CHANGE

Chris and his senior managers made a serious mistake in not giving people adequate *time* to prepare for these major changes on both the emotional and logical level. They should have been given ample time to ask questions, express their doubts and concerns, talk out their worries, and most importantly, have people in a knowledgeable position (perhaps the senior managers themselves) available to answer their questions and reassure them. On the practical level they were not given nearly enough information and support, and certainly did not have the opportunity of talking over their doubts and fears. People always need heavy reassurance and support during major change; this organisation committed a grave error in not providing for this basic human requirement. The consequences long-term were catastrophic because of their shortsightedness in this area.

Next, management totally ignored the emotional needs of the people whom these major changes would most affect. In ignoring this basic need, management paid a very high price indeed at a later stage in discontent, resentment, anger, reduced loyalty and motivation, key personnel leaving, etc. People need to be listened to and heard. They need to know that their feelings are understood and accepted. Above all they need to *feel* they are a part of the change process, not just having it abruptly imposed upon them.

A PRACTICAL METHOD OF ACCEPTING CHANGE

Once the consolidation process has occurred, we are usually able to let go of the old and accept the new. Providing our attitude is right, there is, at this stage, little difficulty in focusing on the future and letting go of the past.

The way in which we can speed up this consolidation process is by firstly accepting our feelings, and not getting uptight about them (this only adds secondary stress). We need to feed in self-talk messages such as 'It's okay to feel the way I am, I'm just experiencing a perfectly natural response to change, so I totally accept my feelings.' I'm not saying we have to like what we are experiencing on the feeling level — there is a big difference between liking and accepting. When we accept, we defuse the intensity of our emotions and therefore move to a point of peacefulness more quickly.

The second step is to express our feelings as fully as possible to somebody whom we can trust, and who will really listen to us. We need to talk out our hopes, fears, dreams, ambitions, joys and anticipation. Both pleasant and unpleasant feelings should be verbally expressed as fully and as often as is necessary. Talking them out once may not be enough; we may have to talk about our feelings a few times in order to speed the adjustment process. If we feel like crying we should allow ourselves to, as this will further move us to the point of consolidation.

Once the levels of logic and emotion have reached an equilibrium, we are ready to move on. At this point it is important that we really focus ahead on the future, accepting the new and letting go of the past. We should avoid any temptation to look back with regret.

If we do not let go and focus ahead we become like a person with a foot on two stools; there is a real danger of us falling into the gap between them. There is always a shutting of emotional doors needed when we move on, and if this process does not occur we are very much at risk from depression. The person who refuses to let go of the old and accept the new, and who keeps focusing back to the past is particularly vulnerable to reactive depression. We cannot stay in a state of such confusion without putting ourselves at risk. So let go of yesterday, and accept the challenges of tomorrow wholeheartedly and without useless regrets.

CUTTING TIES WITH THE OLD AND ACCEPTING THE NEW

It takes time for people to adjust to a new situation, especially in the case of this organisation where staff were simultaneously confronted with two major sets of change. Even at the end of eighteen months some members had still not fully adjusted to the upheaval. Sensitively handled, change can be made easier for people to cope with, and it would have been good management practice to have provided ongoing support for a few months after these major changes in their working life.

EXERCISES

1. Think back to some major changes in your own life. How have you personally coped with change?

2. In the light of what you have now read, do you understand the difference between your reaction to change on the levels of logic and emotion?

3. Have you noticed your differing reactions in these areas when you have been confronted with major change, in both your work and personal life?

4. Have you been aware of the effects of change (on both of these levels) on the people for whom you are responsible?

5. Have you sometimes been surprised at the negative reaction you have received from people who have been confronted by unexpected change?

6. Now that you understand more about the effects of change, how would you help people to adjust to it in the future?

7. How are you yourself helped to adjust to change in your organisation?

8. Do you realise the importance of giving people time to adjust emotionally to change, and of giving them the necessary support throughout this process?

9. If major change is pending within your organisation, either for individuals or for the team, how are you now going to handle it?

TO SUM UP

Sensitively handled, change can be a force for good. Poorly handled, it can be a disaster.

CHAPTER EIGHTEEN

Stress

Lionel was the headmaster of a large secondary school whose staff numbered over a hundred. Having been brought up as the eldest of four brothers and two sisters he found his family background invaluable in helping him interact with the staff he was now responsible for.

On the whole things went very well for Lionel, and the school ran smoothly. Lionel was therefore a little surprised when, half way through the last term, he began encountering a number of problems with his staff. Four of his senior teachers, two of them heads of departments, were off sick for long periods of time with illnesses of a serious nature. This put considerable extra pressure on Lionel and his assistant principal. In addition about a third of his normal teaching and administrative staff seemed to be increasingly unwell, suffering from a range of minor to more serious illnesses.

As if all of this were not enough, he began to notice that many other staff seemed to be on a very short fuse. Some were snappy and irritable and seemed to overreact to issues which they would normally take in their stride. Others just seemed to have lost their motivation and to be achieving only half as much as he had come to expect of them, yet they appeared to be working as hard as ever (if not overworking). Still other people were obviously struggling just to hold themselves together and cope. There seemed to be an atmosphere of tension and negativism prevailing.

Things came to a head a week or two later when Lionel made what he thought was a helpful suggestion to their normally placid, even-tempered head of the music department, only to have her burst into tears, shout at him and walk out. Lionel was flabbergasted. He hadn't a clue what he had said or done wrong. When he eventually found her and tried to sort things out, all he could get from her was, 'It's all too much, Lionel. We're all being pushed far too hard and I can't cope with it any longer.' Seeing how upset she was, Lionel suggested she take the rest of the day off and go home. This brought on more floods of tears, but she was eventually persuaded to do so.

Next day Lionel called a meeting of all his heads of department (those who were not away sick), to ask for their help in trying to find out what was going wrong. He outlined for them the high rate of consistent absenteeism, the excessive number of nuisance-value illnesses, plus some of the more serious ones that seemed to be assailing people on a regular basis. He also expressed his concern about the fact that a large number of staff were becoming downright touchy, if not temperamental. The response he got surprised him. Various senior members of staff at this meeting told him that they had been concerned for quite some time about the very things he outlined, but had not brought it to his attention because they had put it down to a run of bad luck, and they hadn't wanted to worry Lionel further when he was already stretched himself.

After some in-depth discussion, Lionel came to the conclusion that the root cause of the problem was stress. The demands of teaching, the exhaustion that often occurs among teachers in the last term, and various other factors had taken a bigger than usual toll. He determined to do something about it for the future, to prevent a recurrence of the same scenario. He could see that, unfortunately, it was too late to change things very much for this year.

The course of action he took involved sending a questionnaire to all staff to find out how they were feeling and coping, with particular emphasis on their degree of stress. Without exception the response showed that all members of the staff felt stressed, levels varying from mild to heavy but with a large number at the top end of the scale.

His next step was to call another meeting of all senior personnel and ask for their input on how to best handle the situation. They in turn talked to members of their teaching and administrative staff and got their input as well. The upshot of it was that everybody wanted to see the pressure reduced in as many ways as possible. They also wanted training in stress management. Lionel restructured the day-to-day running of the school as much as possible to reduce pressure. He set up more support teams, and increased the frequency of small group meetings among staff to provide more personal support for them all. He also put in a request for additional part-time staff to try and relieve the pressure on the full-timers somewhat. In addition, he took cognisance of their request to learn about stress management, and employed an experienced trainer to come in and present a number of training sessions which all staff would attend in small groups. As can be seen, once aware of the problems this school principal did everything he could to deal with them in the best way he could.

SOME COMMENTS FROM LIONEL'S SCHOOL

I'm not surprised at our finding that stress was at the bottom of this; in retrospect it was so obvious, but at the time you're so pressured and snowed under that you're just fighting to keep your head above water, and so it is not always easy to recognise what is right under your nose. Of course it was stress, but it took Lionel with his determination to investigate what was going on. He involved as many people as possible in giving their input as to the reasons we were in trouble, and to come up with the answer. And as it turns out, the solution.

When you get somebody like Lionel at the helm, you feel confident in them because you know they will do their best for you and you're well aware of their caring and concern. It certainly motivates you to give of your *best. So we're right behind him in what he wants to do. This is just the sort of thing which makes him such a good leader.* (A dean of the high school.)

This has been a really difficult year for me. I've had some exceptionally difficult pupils to deal with, a couple of them really truculent and challenging my authority. I have found this very draining. I have had a lot of support from my immediate senior, and I've also spoken to Lionel about it and he has given me some very useful ideas in handling them, but nevertheless it hasn't been easy. I know the rest of the staff are coping with the same sort of thing, and I think this is one of the reasons why we're all so stressed and are finding it difficult to cope.

However the one bright spot on the horizon is that we've got the best in our principal. He's caring, concerned, but has great strengths as well — he's a wonderful support person for us all really. Also the fact that he recognises our problems and is prepared to do his best to help us with them has given us all quite a boost. (A junior teacher.)

LEARNING TO RECOGNISE STRESS

If we spend our inner resources without replacing them we can become stressed. This is what had happened with most of Lionel's staff because very few of them knew anything about stress, or even that they were in fact stressed. They failed to recognise what was happening to them, and if they had, did not know how to deal with it. Because they had experienced an exceptionally hard year and were becoming overtired, they had depleted their reserves of energy to the point where they were unable to cope with the additional pressure of the end-of-year demands. We can 'pull out all the stops' for a while and get away with it, but if the situation continues unabated for too long then we begin to be ground down by the consistent, unremitting pressure. It's all a question of balance. If we are out of balance for too long we are at risk from stress. Each of the great philosophers down through the ages has said in their own way, 'The key to life lies in balance.' I have always found that when a person has reached a crisis, you can trace back the beginning of the slide downwards to when they got out of balance.

After they had thought about it, and especially after they had taken the stress management course, Lionel and his staff were amazed that they had not recognised what was so obviously happening to them. They are not unusual in this. In industry stress symptoms are often not recognised for what they are, and only too often people reach a point of extreme stress before they (or somebody else) becomes aware of what is happening; the cause is usually excessive and unremitting pressure. In industry relentless pressure often results in serious stress problems; unfortunately it is not until the person really reaches crisis point that it is recognised that stress is at the root of the problem.

SOME COMMON STRESS SYMPTOMS

There are so many stress symptoms on the emotional, behavioural and physical levels that it would be impossible to list them all. Here are a few of the more common ones.

Muscle tension anywhere in the body but particularly in the neck, shoulders, back and stomach
Unreasonable fears, for instance the feeling that a disaster is imminent
Sleep difficulties
Indigestion
Hyperventilation
Shortness of breath
Palpitations (these should always be medically checked)
Feeling faint
Frequent nuisance-value illnesses
Frequent 'silly' accidents or mistakes
Chronic tiredness
Touchiness and over-sensitivity
Being snappy and on a short fuse
Irritability and/or aggressive behaviour
Ongoing feelings of apathy
Tearfulness, or a desire to cry
Blood pressure higher than normal
Tension headaches
Upset stomach
Change in appetite
Frequent waking during the night
Difficulty in falling asleep
Depression
Withdrawal
Poor judgement
Illogical thinking
Inability to concentrate
Short-term memory lapses

General loss of enjoyment of life
Failure to enjoy what previously gave feelings of satisfaction and fulfilment
Loss of sense of humour
Difficulty in decision-making
Flitting from job to job and completing nothing
Rigid behaviour
Loss or reduction in libido
A feeling of being wound up like a tight spring
A feeling of choking
Altered bowel habits
Feeling of weight on the chest
Unexplained aches and pains
Clenched jaw

These are just a few of the more common stress symptoms; there are many more too numerous to mention here. When Lionel and his staff thought about it they found that between the lot of them they had a very high proportion of those listed!

LEARN TO LISTEN TO YOUR BODY

One of the important things Lionel and his staff learnt in the stress management seminar, and which would be a safeguard for them in the future when the pressure was really on, was to listen to their body and learn to identify their early warning stress symptoms. I believe that we all have an early warning stress symptom which is unique to us. It can be in the form of any of the above — or may be something apart from those listed here. It occurs in the following way.

Whenever pressure becomes too great for us, we experience a particular stress symptom. There may well be more than one, but this particular one is always there when we are stressed, and it usually presents in advance of whatever other stress symptoms we may also experience. For example, I may experience a feeling of tension across the back of the neck and shoulders when I become stressed. If I ignore it I will then get a headache. If I ignore that I will then perhaps experience a feeling of weight on the chest, and after that I may feel weepy. If I ignore all these I may also experience palpitations. However, regardless of all of these other stress symptoms, I nearly always first experience the feeling of tension in the area of the neck and shoulders.

If we listen to what our body is trying to tell us, we need never travel too far down the stress trail. By throwing out these early warning stress symptoms, our body is trying to let us know that we have reached the point where stress has changed from being beneficial to us (*eustress,* which means good stress) to being destructive. The trick is always to act quickly on our early warning stress symptoms. We experience an early warning stress symptom when the degree of arousal becomes excessive; this indicates that the body is telling us of the need for change. It is important to know and identify our own tolerance to stress before reaching this point.

Wisely used, stress will motivate us and work for us. However, if we get past the point of best performance stress will cause us to perform less well. We may, in fact, feel distressed. Going over this safety margin into the distress area too many times leads to what is commonly termed 'burnout'. When we are in real danger our bodies automatically trigger a fight or flight response; this is good because it enables us to act quickly and strongly in the appropriate way to get out of danger and preserve our life. Unfortunately this response is very often inappropriately triggered by emotions or unpleasant memories, or even by unrealistic expectations of oneself. If this happens too frequently burnout will quickly follow. This is exactly what was happening with the staff at this busy secondary school, with all the unrelenting demands which were made upon them in the final term.

THE DIFFERENCE BETWEEN PRESSURE AND STRESS

It is important to note the difference between pressure and stress. Pressure will not necessarily cause us stress, but a lot of stress (especially if prolonged) will certainly damage us. Pressure is what happens to us externally, stress is what we experience internally. However, stress may occur even when the person may not, in fact, be overworked but *feels* that they are. Demands (even a few) throw them into a state of inner panic. Stress is here operating in the absence of undue pressure. Another example would be when a person is stressed because they cannot let go of work, even when they go home and should be relaxing and focusing on other things. A person who can forget their work when they go home is merely experiencing pressure, even though they may have been overworked during the day. We all have a different stress threshold which is as unique to us as our individuality. The way we respond to stress is also very individual. Hereditary factors, childhood conditioning, our psychological and physiological makeup, perception of things and experience all have an influence. This is why one person can take a lot of pressure and not become stressed, while another (who actually has very little pressure in their lives) may constantly be stressed. The good news is that, with all the education regarding keeping stress under control, it is true that we can consistently increase our stress tolerance level over a period of time.

Once they had learnt these simple anti-stress keys, Lionel and his staff determined to put them into practice to see if they could avoid reaching the high stress state too many of them had experienced in the last term.

It is of great value for the leaders in industry to recognise the primary stress symptoms, and know how to reduce stress and keep it manageable. They need to do so not only for their own sake (the higher you go the more pressure you wear), but also so that they can be aware of the effect stress can have upon the people for whom they are responsible. I believe that it is an important part of the leader's 'bag-of-skills' that they know and understand something about the nature of stress.

SOME POINTERS TO KEEPING STRESS UNDER CONTROL

Identifying our early warning stress symptom (often called our best friend) and keeping in touch with what our body is trying to tell us is of great value to us. On recognising the early symptoms we can quickly take reverse action to reduce stress.

It is useful to remember the maxim 'When the mind is tired, work the body; when the body is tired, work the mind.' If fatigue occurs and we are becoming stressed through doing mental work, it is advisable to take a minute or two out, clear the mind completely, and do something physical. The very act of changing one's occupation is in itself a stress breaker. Another way in which we can bring some balance into the situation is by stopping and stretching and moving our arms and legs and back in a stretching motion. Yet another good tension-breaker is to gaze out of the window focusing on a cloud formation, or the movement of trees, and completely clear the mind. When we do so we mentally switch from one gear (logical thinking) to another (creative thinking), and thereby rest and refresh the mind. Unfortunately many offices nowadays do not have outside windows. If this is the case I would suggest you get a large seascape or landscape poster, pin it on the wall by your desk, and just stand up and gaze at it for a moment. A good way of knowing whether or not the picture is right for you is to ask yourself the question 'Can I see myself in that scene? Can I walk around in it?'

Just to take a few minutes out and go outside and walk around the building is also an excellent way of replenishing one's nervous energies and breaking the build-up of stress as it is occurring. The reverse principle applies if one is becoming fatigued or stressed through physical exercise. Do something different. Sit down and read a set of instructions or study something for a few moments. Balance can be achieved very quickly by simply reversing one's normal way of functioning for a moment or two. The trick is to break the stress *as it is building,* and not to let it gain in momentum. Stress is easy to deal with if it is dealt with speedily, but it's a different thing altogether if it builds up to a high level. Most people work in unhealthy way, mentally tightening their belt and pushing themselves on further instead of stopping, having a stress break of a minute or two when necessary, and then carrying on. Consequently their level of efficiency declines. If people would only learn to pace themselves, they would find that they would achieve much better overall results; they would keep their level of efficiency and concentration higher through working in this way. The overall result would be noticeable within a short time.

A USEFUL ONE-MINUTE STRESS BREAKER

Here is a one-minute stress breaker which Lionel and his staff were taught and urged to apply about four times a day, as well as whenever they felt that stress was building up. I feel that this should be taught and used in the workforce generally, because it is such a valuable tool in reducing stress quickly. It involves diaphragmatic breathing, which has long been used to aid relaxation, and it goes as follows.

Place both your hands with fingertips touching just under your rib cage. Breathe slowly and deeply pushing your diaphragm *out* as you breathe in, and pulling it gently back *in* as you breathe out. Notice that your fingertips part slightly on your inward breath. Diaphragmatic breathing in a slow, deep, rhythmical way triggers a relaxation response. It is possible to very much add to the effectiveness of the exercise by doing a little creative visualisation as well. Once you have mastered the technique of pushing out the diaphragm as you breathe in, and pulling it in as you breathe out, add the following.

Picture yourself breathing in a white mist of relaxation on your inner breath, and releasing tension (gathered from all centres of the body) as a darker mist on your outer breath. The mind controls the body, so you can see how this will make the exercise even more effective. Do not continue breathing this way for a long period of time while you are unused to it, as you may become dizzy. Rather, start off very gradually, building up to breathing like this for a minute or two. This exercise is one of the most effective tension breakers there is. It will reduce stress very quickly and should be used on a regular basis throughout the day. To break tension by breathing this way for even a minute will be very therapeutic.

BALANCE

Another very important aspect of keeping stress under control involves getting balance in one's life. Lionel and his team learnt that one of the greatest stress beaters was to keep maintaining balance in all its forms — between work and play, time alone and interaction with other people, mental and physical activity, logical thinking and creative thinking. They were advised to do some daily relaxation, which involved listening to a relaxation tape (see page 206), and were also told that no matter how busy and pressured they became, they should find time for exercise on a daily basis. Even a fast half-hour walk breaks tension and helps mind and body to balance out. It is also essential to have creative hobbies and activities as a contrast to the continual pressure of work. The busier one is, the more these things are necessary. Sometimes it takes major rethinking and restructuring to include them in one's life, but nevertheless the pay-offs from doing so can result in a much reduced stress level. It is to their credit that they took this advice seriously.

Earlier I mentioned the necessity of having time and space for oneself. The only time we really recharge our batteries is when we are by ourselves. People in busy occupations (especially where there is continual involvement with people) need to have time alone to simply allow periods of quiet and to indulge in the state of 'just being'. This is a way of replenishing energies. It is also important that we create a state of better balance by allowing our brain to go into a resting and creative mode, in contrast to the demands of continually thinking logically and making day-to-day decisions.

We tap into our deeper consciousness by daydreaming or just enjoying the beauties of our environment, doing handcrafts, whittling wood, gardening and so on (providing these things do not demand intense concentration). We benefit when we allow ourselves to indulge in activities which do not demand being mentally alert; it is a way of attaining mental balance. It is at times like these (and as a result of allowing the space in which to have times like these) that we think creatively, and will come up with deeper insights, ideas and sudden flashes of inspiration.

Scheduling these activities (or rather non-activities) into our lives helps us to create a very necessary and healthy balance, as a result of which our whole body benefits. Having the achieving of balance as a guiding principle in our lives is one of the most important ways of keeping stress under control.

IMPORTANT ADDITIONAL KEYS TO BREAKING STRESS

Another key to handling stress which Lionel and the team learnt was to set limits wisely, that is, by saying no, and not overcommitting themselves. Many of us have difficulty with this, overcommitting ourselves when it would have been far more appropriate to give a polite refusal. We need to learn to balance wisdom with the desire to give and to please others. Giving ourselves permission to have time to ourselves each day means that we ultimately have more energy to offer other people.

EXPRESSING FEELINGS

The staff at Lionel's school had not realised the importance of accepting and expressing their feelings, and were 'sitting on these' and silently suffering. There is an old saying that the body has to express what *we* fail to — and it will do so. For instance, if you are angry and upset about something but fail to deal with it by expressing your feelings, your body will later have to deal with it. So perhaps two days later you may have a headache or a digestive upset — a very common reaction to unexpressed negative emotions. Once the group learnt how to accept and express their feelings in positive and non-destructive ways, they made marked progress.

In addition Lionel set up support groups among the staff, so that they could air their frustrations and problems in a safe and understanding environment. Though members of staff had tried to give each other support throughout the year, and certainly were willing to listen to each other's problems and gripes, their busy schedules and demanding jobs prevented them from providing the amount of regular support for each other that was really necessary. It was therefore important that the opportunity for listening and supporting was made available in a more structured way.

Support groups were set up consisting of a few people who related well to each other and who did similar work, and time was scheduled for them to meet on a weekly basis (or more often if somebody was experiencing a major problem). Results from setting this new scheme into action showed up almost immediately in the form of reduced stress, and a lift in the general emotional climate. As one senior member of staff said, 'It's hard to describe what the setting-up of support groups has done, it's a nebulous thing, but all I can say is that everybody seems to feel more secure and certainly a lot happier. Knowing you've got your own people caring about you does wonders for you psychologically.'

THE RIGHT ATTITUDE TO COUNTER STRESS

Another key to keeping stress under control is attitude. This group learnt how important it was to maintain a positive attitude in the midst of all the pressure they were experiencing, and to keep things in perspective. They learnt that their mood could very quickly be elevated or depressed by the way they allowed themselves to think when things got tough. They were also made aware of the dangers of having a rigid attitude and an unrealistic expectation of themselves and of other people. They discovered how perfectionism can lead to compulsive and obsessive behaviour (with all of its damaging consequences), and recognised the dangers of trying to do everything to perfection. When one does this on a consistent basis the end consequence is invariably an unacceptable level of stress.

DAILY RELAXATION

Lionel's group were also encouraged to commit themselves to the practice of daily relaxation (in the form of a ten to fifteen minute exercise applied daily), and some of them agreed to do this at a regular time each day in a group. Lionel provided a room in which they could do so. Having learnt how to apply one-minute tension breakers (the breathing exercise previously given) and their value in defusing stress quickly, they agreed to apply it on a regular basis throughout the day and whenever necessary.

MANAGING OURSELVES AND OUR TIME

Disorganisation creates stress; when we feel out of control of ourselves and our immediate environment (in other words we are disorganised) we can expect to experience an increase in tension. There is no greater exacerbator of stress than feeling that one's life, and therefore one's work, is out of control and that too many commitments are taking over too much time. Many members of the group opted to take a time management course and to put into practice the skills they learnt from this.

These are only a few of the keys which were taught to Lionel and his staff, but nevertheless they are important ones. I would, however, urge everybody, especially those in any kind of leadership or management role, to take the opportunity to learn all they can about stress, both for their own sake and the sake of those working for them. Lionel found, as did his staff, that when he learnt about this important aid to modern day living he was able to very quickly identify stress warning symptoms in the people for whom he was responsible. The advantages of being able to do so are obvious. He was able to understand what was happening, bring it to the staff member or student's attention, and was therefore in a better position to help them deal with it.

Lionel also recognised the need to seek support for himself and to be with supportive people. The greater the responsibility we carry the more we need to have a team of supportive and positive people around us, and the more we need to have built-in support systems. Lionel realised that he was not getting sufficient of either, and so he set about rectifying this situation.

Many a manager or leader in industry has been confused and dismayed at the reaction of some of their staff from time to time, not realising the extent to which stress can change our behaviour. Knowledge *is* power, and once we recognise the stress factor we are in a much better position to offer help.

EXERCISES

1. Recall as many as possible of the symptoms of stress.

2. Which of these symptoms do you recognise as sometimes occurring in yourself?

3. How is your own stress level at this time?

4. In the light of what you have read, should your stress level start to rise what would you do about it?

5. Which stress symptoms have you observed in other people? Are some of them occurring among people you work with now?

6. If you should find that members of your staff are becoming stressed how would you handle it?

7. What practical support and help would you offer your staff in dealing with this problem?

8. What can you do now, at this present time, to try and keep stress to a manageable level in your workforce?

TO SUM UP

Not all stress is destructive. Remember eustress (good stress). Keeping the balance in our work, life, and immediate environment will help to create this state of eustress — a state which motivates people, causes them to enjoy their work, and stimulates them to better performance. Other factors, such as creating a positive working environment, praising, encouraging, and working to achieve a good team spirit and a feeling of team support and unity, will also help create this desirable state. If there is sufficient challenge and stimulation, combined with a feeling of being a vital member of the team whose opinion and input are valued, a person will be more likely to experience this state of good stress.

Conversely, anyone who feels they are just a cog in the wheel, not valued for themselves and for the part they play, is more likely to experience stress. It takes insight and thought to create a positive working environment, but it is always worth striving to do so because excessive stress demotivates people, whereas positive stress will motivate them towards a higher level of functioning and overall achievement. Most people enjoy the feeling of giving of their best, and the satisfaction and fulfilment which comes from getting results.

CHAPTER NINETEEN

Mistake-making, delegating and other important leadership keys

Dean was the manager of a hotel in a large international chain. He had been promoted to his job at the comparatively young age of 36, because of his exceptional business acumen and managerial skills. He was recognised in the hotel world as a young man who was going places, and therefore somebody to be watched. Though he had such obvious abilities and was highly skilled at what he did, Dean nevertheless had some shortcomings in certain areas of people management, mainly in being too much of a perfectionist, failing to delegate — thereby limiting his own growth and performance — and mishandling situations when members of his staff made mistakes.

As can be imagined this 700-bed hotel needed a well-functioning team to keep it running smoothly and showing a profit. The pressure of trying to stay ahead in the competitive tourist industry and keep beds and conference facilities fully utilised was beginning to tell on Dean.

A perfectionist himself, Dean did not find it easy to handle other people's mistakes. He could be relied upon to take a negative, critical stance, often bawling out the mistake-maker in front of other members of the staff. He brooked no excuses and would not listen to explanations. Often he would proceed to criticise the person as well as the mistake. This caused a lot of resentment and frustration among his staff; as a consequence he failed to get the full co-operation and willingness to help that he so earnestly and frequently sought of people.

Dean had a horror of making mistakes and being found wanting himself, and this was at the root of why he was so intolerant and aggressive when he saw others making mistakes. Only too often when we overreact to certain qualities in others we are simply reflecting what we fear in ourselves, but Dean did not recognise this. As a result of his extremely negative attitude towards making mistakes, people tried to cover their errors as much as possible; they would not report things going wrong until it was too late to do much about it. This of course quite often had serious consequences, and the repercussions cost Dean much, both in money and wasted time and energy.

Linked with his horror of mistake-making (and as a consequence of it), came a general lack of trust that anybody else could do things as well as he could. This attitude was evident to his staff and contributed to the less than happy atmosphere which pervaded the hotel. It also caused many of his key people to experience a lack of confidence. Not believing that anybody else could really make decisions or handle situations as well as he could, Dean was failing to delegate as he should.

People who were trained to cope with responsibilities, to carry additional responsibility when necessary, and who were able to make day-to-day decisions regarding the running of the hotel, were prevented from doing so by Dean's failure to trust them. He simply would not delegate responsibility. He was often heard to say 'I like to keep my finger on the pulse,' but keeping his finger on the pulse meant, in fact, interfering, overruling decisions previously made, blocking what others were trying to do, and generally not allowing his quite capable staff to make their own decisions and organise themselves. Carrying so much of the responsibility himself, however, meant that he was constantly stressed out, irascible and difficult to deal with. It also had the effect of demotivating many of his staff, especially his key personnel who saw themselves as being stuck in a groove, unable to progress and gain further experience as long as Dean remained manager.

Although he did not realise it, Dean was actually working against himself. The more he demotivated his people and knocked their confidence through his attitude and failure to delegate, the more he was effectively isolating himself from their support.

Managers like Dean are effectively painting themselves into a corner. They become unable to rely on other people to assume any responsibility, because their people are simply not experienced enough. When managers or leaders put themselves in a position where they are systematically isolating themselves from their key personnel, they are playing a dangerous game, and one which in time will undoubtedly have repercussions for them.

As is common with many hardworking perfectionists, Dean was also exhibiting an inability to stand back and objectively assess situations. He was too stressed to be able to see the overall picture and became more and more obsessed with the immediate details and decisions demanding his attention. Like a person who can only see one piece of the jigsaw puzzle, the one immediately in front of their nose, and cannot see where all pieces fit together to form the total picture, Dean was so hooked into the day-to-day running of things that he was unable to see and find clear direction. This is a common consequence of a perfectionist attitude and a failure to delegate.

Dean knew he was not coping well, but the thought of seeking help was threatening to him (again a common reaction of the perfectionist). He therefore dismissed the thought very quickly and firmly. Nothing threatened him more than the thought or suggestion that he hadn't 'got it all together' and wasn't functioning at a high level of efficiency.

Again in common with many demanding perfectionists, Dean had long since lost his sense of humour, and with the exception of occasions when somebody else would make a fool of themselves, he no longer had the ability to laugh. He could not see the humour in the minor day-to-day happenings around him, and he certainly could not laugh at himself — always a sign of high stress.

Dean has so much going for him with his good business acumen and lively, quick intelligence, that it is unfortunate that his mishandling of his staff and present inability to lead in a positive way are undermining all that he is trying to achieve. So far he has managed, through his business expertise and experience, to keep things on an even keel. However, with the way he is consistently alienating himself from the personnel within the hotel, it is doubtful whether he will be able to maintain the level of success he has enjoyed to date. Dean's style of management is too short-sighted to bring about lasting loyalty and commitment.

SOME COMMENTS ON DEAN'S LEADERSHIP

Dean is a good manager in many ways and I've learned a lot from observing his style, but he's not a good people person really. So how he's got to rise so high in a service industry, I don't know. He can be charming enough to guests, and he's good at smoothing things over when there are problems with them, but he's far too hard on his staff at times. He can be critical to the point of being ridiculous. You have to be pretty perfect to work around Dean. Mind you, he's a perfectionist himself, and sometimes I think he gets himself too stressed because of this. I have seen him actually shaking when things were going wrong, or when he makes a mistake himself. The charming suave everything-under-control front is all for the hotel owners and guests.

Most of us don't go to him with problems because we know he's going to overreact and probably blame us, so problems, mistakes and difficulties get hidden as much as possible around this place. As I said, he's basically a good manager as far as tasks go, but I'd in no way call him a good leader. (One of Dean's office staff.)

I admire Dean in many respects, and I've learnt quite a lot from him. He's good at finding solutions to management problems, but with people he is probably too quick and too impatient, and gets himself in such a stew. He seems to regard it as a personal attack if anybody makes a mistake or fails to do their job perfectly 100 percent of the time.

I also wish he would allow us to assume greater responsibility. He even rings up or comes in on his day off to take control of what is happening. You feel you have no authority, and that the personnel here are not going to take you seriously because they know that what you say is likely to be countermanded in an hour's time.

Also he has to make all the decisions himself. That's a very short-sighted policy too, because the guy can't be everywhere at once. The joke of it is that because he's so overworked and is stretching himself too far, he's starting to make more and more mistakes himself. I guess it's a consequence of trying to run the whole ship single-handed.

I don't know that I will actually stay here too much longer, in fact I'm already looking elsewhere for a vacancy at my level. I know I could learn a lot more from Dean, and I've already learnt quite a lot from him about how to run a huge complex like this efficiently, but it's got to the stage where I feel he's limiting me. If he won't let me do my job properly because he keeps interfering, and won't let me have any say in decision-making, I don't know that I can really progress much further. (Dean's assistant manager.)

DELEGATE OR ISOLATE

It is a very short-sighted policy indeed to fail to delegate where it is appropriate to do so. Managers or leaders who don't delegate are creating a rod for their own back. In fact anyone in this position who fails to pass on responsibility to others as they move up the corporate ladder can be compared to a person who is endeavouring to climb the ladder while still having anchors slung around their ankles. They will be held back (and in fact bogged down) by the weight of too much decision-making, and the inappropriate carrying of unnecessary responsibility. Anybody in this position who is any good at their job knows that to become a really efficient performer they must almost work themselves out of a job. The higher one goes the more the demands on one's ability to think deeply and creatively, and to see the whole picture — the wood rather than the trees. Add to this the need for vision and you have a weighty brief for anyone. Having the ability to let go of much of the detail work and day-to-day running of the business in order to step back and see what is actually occurring is of paramount importance. It is the only way the leader can have overall broader and clearer vision. To perform efficiently and well the person at this level of responsibility must have the good sense to delegate as much as they can, and to train others to take up the responsibility. They need to invest time and energy in order to give them the confidence to do so. Our most precious commodity is ourselves (and this involves our ability to think creatively); our second most important commodity is our time. The efficient leader uses both wisely and well.

A burnt-out leader is of no value to anybody. Dean was obviously already on this path; he was in fact beginning to make obvious and unnecessary mistakes because he was trying to carry too much of the load himself. He was also in danger of losing key personnel. Nobody who is ambitious, capable and motivated to climb the ladder in business is going to allow their progress to be blocked for any length of time. Consequently Dean was in real danger of losing the people who could most help and support him. He was in fact isolating himself through his own unwillingness to trust his key personnel. This is a serious mistake which many leaders make.

Perhaps you have heard the story of the managing director who had to stay behind after everybody had gone home, in order to do the office boy's job of tidying-up, because he didn't feel it was ever done well enough (a true story). It takes trust and confidence in people on the way up to delegate, but unless one is prepared to do so, these people will never have a chance to prove their worth. Perhaps just as importantly, they will never have the opportunity of developing the confidence to 'grow into the job'. If they did not have the ability to do so, they should never have been appointed to that position in the first place. Having made the decision to give them a position of responsibility, it behoves the leader to build their confidence and encourage them to test their wings. Not to do so is to highlight areas of inadequacy within the leader. Long-term it is also an extremely short-sighted policy — as Dean is on the point of finding out.

MISTAKES ARE BUT GROWTH STEPS

It will be obvious that Dean's overreaction to his staff's mistakes was simply a reflection of his own fear of making mistakes. As is common with many people in the perfectionist syndrome, Dean felt threatened by any performance (his own or other people's) which was less than perfect. He was obviously making a very bad mistake himself. In fact, for all his fear of mistake-making, this would be his biggest error. Making mistakes is one of the greatest ways of learning there is. If the mistake is handled in a positive way, we learn from it, and as a result grow a little more. It would be fair to say that there is almost nothing that will have the same learning impact as the making of mistakes.

Where a safe, accepting climate is created, people feel secure enough to approach the person they are answerable to and to say 'Hey, I'm afraid I've blued. I have made a big mistake. This is what I have done . . . ' The wise leader encourages people to be honest and upfront about their mistakes, and to bring them to the attention of the person who can help them deal with them earlier rather than later. This way a mistake often has minimal consequences: left to grow and develop, the consequences are usually of a far more serious nature.

MISTAKES MEAN THE PERSON IS MOVING

If a person is making mistakes it shows they are moving. What the leader or manager has to fear is not the fact that people are making mistakes, but rather the situation where no mistakes are being made. This shows that people have either given up trying, are seriously demotivated, or are so in fear of the consequences that they will not extend themselves *for fear of* making mistakes. Often it is simply that people have become demotivated to the point where they will avoid being put in a position where they have to make any decisions or try to take any additional responsibility for anything. This can be summed up under the heading of a general opting-out wherever possible. This is not only negative, it is also extremely destructive to the organisation as a whole.

Once a mistake is made and a lesson learnt, it is time to move on. It is a totally unfair exercise to remind people of previous mistakes. Doing so is destructive and will have a very negative effect upon them. A mistake made and recognised is history, and should be treated as such.

OTHER AREAS TO ADDRESS

Other areas in which Dean fell short and set a bad example were in not seeking personal support and in failing to involve his staff in day-to-day decisions which affected them personally. How can they possibly learn, grow and become more experienced (let alone take on more responsibility) if he continues to act in this way? It will be very difficult for them to get it right until they have been given the opportunity of being involved on a personal level. Dean is also sending across, loudly and clearly, the message that it is a sign of weakness to ask for support or to show that one needs it. Without realising it Dean is actually breaking down his own team structure.

STEP BACK, RELAX AND ASSESS THE TOTAL SITUATION

Because of his high stress and perfectionist tendencies, Dean was also failing to adopt a basic leadership principle. He was not sitting back and assessing the total situation. He was in fact far too hooked by detail, and so was not objectively assessing the situation. There is no quicker way to lose direction than to fall into this pitfall, and if a leader loses direction then he or she has no vision to share with their staff, and cannot help them maintain direction.

Imagine what would happen on a football field if there was no team plan and co-operation, and if each player was playing only for themselves. Dean was undervaluing his team, and attempting to win the game single-handedly. In fact it was only his quick mind and overall experience which enabled him to efficiently run the hotel as well as he did, but his was a short-term way of functioning.

If he is to rescue the situation, Dean needs to be far more flexible in both his attitude and functioning. He must start training his managers and key people to lead, but first he must alter his own leadership style to be far more positive. Dealing constructively with mistake-making, being willing to delegate, and showing more confidence in and support of people are prerequisites before any change can be effected.

EXERCISES

1. What are Dean's areas of strength? of weakness?

2. How do you handle your own mistake-making?

3. What is your attitude towards other people making mistakes?

4. Are you threatened by the fact that you and other people make mistakes?

5. Are you in a position to delegate work and responsibility and do you do so?

6. If you are failing to do so partially or totally, why is this?

7. Are you recognising the need to delegate as you assume more responsibility and climb your career ladder?

8. Do you seek support for yourself, and encourage your staff to also seek support and give it to each other?

9. Are you flexible in your functioning, or is there only one way of doing things and that's your way?

10. To the best of your ability, do you endeavour to create an accepting and positive climate in your workplace?

TO SUM UP

Sony chairman Akio Morita says 'American managers are too concerned about short-term profits and too little concerned about their workers.' Are we?

When asked the question 'How does Apple do it?', Stephen Jobs, co-founder of the brilliantly successful company Apple Computer Inc, said, 'Well, we hire really great people and we create an environment where people can make mistakes and grow.' Should we take a leaf?

We all have a tendency to avoid risks. Let's face it. Failure hurts! Every time you try something new you run the risk of failing. But, ironically, risk avoidance carries the worst risk any person or organisation can take. It is the surest guarantee of boredom, frustration, stagnation and ultimate failure.
(Michael Le Boeuf)

CHAPTER TWENTY

Essential keys to being an exceptional leader and manager

1. Develop your personal leadership qualities.

• Perhaps the most important quality of all is to *believe in yourself* and in your ability to lead and manage well. This means having the sure knowledge that you are *capable* of being an excellent leader and manager. It involves acting in a way that fits with your belief, even if this means acting a little in advance of where you are actually at. Stop sometimes and ask yourself the question 'What would a really good leader do in this situation?' Then it's a matter of acting as you believe a good leader would. In a sense it's a process comparable to a child putting their feet in adult shoes and not only acting as an adult would, but knowing that in time they will grow to fit those shoes. Sometimes we have to act as we wish to become in order to become.

• Closely related to belief in self is *positive thinking*. Regardless of the skills you have you will never reach your potential as a leader until you begin to think positively. When we think in a positive way we begin to make positive things happen.

Positive thinking programmes our deeper consciousness to work for us, and automatically steers us in the right direction to enable us to achieve our goals. Through our thinking we can condition ourselves to succeed or fail. Confidence and positive thinking go hand in hand, so if you want to remove the blocks which are preventing you from functioning at the best possible level, ensure that you pay attention to the art of thinking positively. We are continually programming our inner computer to work for or against us. Are you your own worst enemy or your own best friend?

- Success is simply the result of *the cultivation of good habits* which you are daily living by. Failure is often simply being governed by bad habits. If you do something three times you have the beginnings of a habit. After three weeks a habit pattern has usually become established. From this point on you will be likely to repeat your action without giving it much thought. It takes a conscious decision to then go back and change your way of functioning, once you have established the habit of doing things in a certain way. You can see how easy it is to fall into bad habits which will then proceed to work against you and begin to hold you back. It takes just a little more effort right at the beginning to establish good habits — and then let them work for you.

- Set the pace, and *lead with your calm, positive attitude,* and you will find that others pick up the vibes and will follow suit. The good leader can be one of the gang, but knows when to take a step forward and put on their leader's hat. In other words they know how and when to assume overall responsibility and to make decisions and set limits. This is what being a leader is all about. A leader not only sets the scene and pace — *they lead.*

- *Maintain the highest ethics.* It is more important for the leader to be respected than liked, but respect usually brings liking anyway. Maintain your integrity by keeping promises. To ensure that you do not forget a promise, keep a section in your diary or yearly work planner especially for promises. Write them down as soon as you make them.

  Do not either gossip, listen to, or encourage gossiping. This is like an insidious, creeping disease which quickly undermines morale in the workforce. Nothing sours the climate quicker than gossip and back-biting. Discourage it by making positive statements about the person being attacked, point out their strengths, or else change the subject, or even simply walk away. If you as the leader set the example, others will follow.

• *Keep your sense of humour* — especially when things get tough. A sense of humour breaks stress, and is one of the greatest weapons we have for keeping things in perspective and restoring the balance. Learn to laugh at yourself and at the many things which go wrong. Sometimes it gets to the stage where the only thing left to do is laugh; if you can do so you immediately break the tension both in yourself and in the general working environment. If we can see the funny side of things we will be better able to cope with the disasters which sometimes seem to bombard us. Other people will take their cue from you and will quickly get the message that 'This is nothing we can't cope with, if we keep it in perspective.' Laughter also keeps you healthier by stimulating the endocrine system to work more efficiently for you.

• *Be generous.* Go the extra mile for people. This includes both staff and clients. You will find that it really pays off to do so. I know one managing director of a large firm whose staff are utterly loyal and committed to him and would be prepared to go the extra mile for *him* — especially when the pressure is on.

This man takes time out of his busy schedule to visit his employees' children or spouses when they are in hospital, bearing an armful of gifts. This is the sort of thing that really speaks to people. It's not what you say, but what you are and what you do which says it all. The basic principle here is, if you want to get — give! Incidentally this M.D. doesn't have to ask people to work longer or harder when the pressure is on. They just do it.

• *Be full of compassion* — but always dispense it with wisdom. This shows real strength and is the hallmark of a great leader. It is also compatible with firm leadership, and shows balance in leading.

• *Be prepared to be a risk-taker,* but do your homework first. If you wish to be successful you are going to have to take calculated risks. Doing so is the price we pay for being successful, so don't fear risk-taking. You will find throughout history (and in industry too) that calculated risk-taking is a characteristic of successful people, and real leaders.

- *Have integrity.* Don't ever betray confidences. It is the quickest way to lose people's trust. It can take months if not years to rebuild credibility.

- *Perseverance, consistency and commitment.* Success can be dependent on many factors, some more important than others. I would rate these three as right at the top of the list.

  Often it is only by hanging in there and persevering, especially when things appear not to be working or are really tough, that you will find a way and be successful. There's many a genius or extremely talented person who has fallen by the wayside and never succeeded simply because they got bored or gave up because of the difficulties and did not persevere. This little word cannot be given too much emphasis.

  So many people do not know how to work consistently. They work in fits and starts. By not working within a framework of balance they drain themselves too much, or eventually burn themselves out. The best way to maintain overall quality and to work efficiently is to do so steadily and consistently. It's the consistent stayers who prove to be successful in the end.

  Commitment ties in very closely with consistency and perseverance, as it implies staying the course to achieve your goals or a certain result. Commitment involves pulling out all stops to achieve a predetermined goal. The committed person will usually get results in the end through giving generously of time and energy, and applying willpower to the achievement of goals.

- *Learn how to think creatively.* By tapping into the deeper creative processes we can use the brain more fully and develop the ability to think laterally. There are courses available which will teach you how to do so. I have found that even people who are strongly in favour of logical thinking have been amazed at how much better and more creative their answers to problems are once they have learnt how to access the fuller brain.

  If you don't start thinking creatively (and have your people do the same) you will end up doing what you have always done just because it is a habit. You may well always go for the quick-fix or more surface answer, and stick with the most obvious and easiest way of solving the problem. Both leader and team need to break out of this rigid mould.

- *It is better to be respected than liked.* A person who is liked may not necessarily be respected, but a person who is respected often becomes liked. A part of wearing the leader's hat involves being unpopular at times, because you have to make unpopular decisions or go against what the majority wants (usually for the overall good of the organisation). Often in this situation, you are not able to disclose the reasons why you have to stand against the popular wish.

  You will not be popular all of the time — accept this as a fact of life, but if you maintain your own integrity by doing what is right for the individual and the organisation, then you will win respect. We do not need to have everybody like and love us, but we do need to win the respect of people.

2. Learn to organise time to your advantage.

- Get balance into your working day by having a *quiet time* when you can do your most creative and innovative thinking. This means that you will have to arrange a time when others know not to interrupt you unless in an emergency. You deserve and need this period of time on a daily basis. Setting aside time for a period of quiet planning, reflection and solitary thinking each day helps you to get your priorities right and put things in perspective. If you fail to do so you are likely to just get busier, while at the same time working less effectively. Encourage others in responsible positions to do the same. It may be that you have to shut your door at the same time each day for others to get used to your 'thinking time'. Or it may be that you have to adopt a buddy-system and arrange with your colleagues to cover for each other so that you can all have a little priority thinking time. The busier you are the more you need it. Do it!

- *Being busy does not mean efficiency.* If you're too busy you may not really be working well. What is the problem? Are you failing to delegate? Are you failing to organise yourself and your work to achieve the best results? Are you failing to manage your time well? Are you failing to set your limits, and allowing yourself to be continually overloaded? Sit down quietly and analyse what is causing you to be too busy, and thereby preventing you from working efficiently and well. Being too busy causes people to lose focus and direction.

Ask yourself two final questions: Are you disorganised? Is the source from whom you receive your work disorganised and functioning inefficiently? Whatever the answers, take appropriate action!

• *Slice up your 'time pie'.* Draw a wheel of how you spend your time each day so that you will know what you do with it. This is a free-hand drawing, not a mathematical equation so don't get hooked into technicalities. Simply divide a wheel up into the time segments, heading each segment according to a job you do in the course of the day, for example, telephoning. The segment matches the time spent on each aspect of your work. You may find that half your wheel is headed 'Meetings', in which case you can see at a glance that you are spending far too much time at meetings. This is a very good way of literally seeing exactly what you are doing with your time.

Next draw up a wheel and divide it in segments which relate to how you think you *should* be spending your time. Now compare the two. As you are able to, make the changes necessary to spend your time on the things it should be spent on. This drawing exercise will start you thinking and then moving. You will see from it what your greatest time-wasters are, and if you are doing tasks which are relatively unimportant. You will also see where you should be spending your time. From this exercise ask yourself which activities demand more time, and which need less time. Also what can be eliminated or passed on to others?

• *Is it a want or is it a need?* This question can make the difference between giving of yourself and your time in a positive way when appropriate and necessary, or falling into a compassion trap. Many people would like to waste your time and have you smooth their path and do things for them which they are perfectly capable of doing for themselves (perhaps with a little encouragement and support from you). We all have many wants but few real needs. We do have a responsibility to meet real needs, for instance when someone genuinely can't manage something, or is very stressed or overloaded. But not to meet everybody's wants. When confronted with many demands, pause and ask yourself 'Is it a want or is it a need?' It's a great way to sort out the wheat from the chaff.

- *Lack of planning is a pathway to disaster.* Certainly we should be flexible, and if the situation or circumstances alter we should be prepared to change, but we must have an overall plan to work to, otherwise we will be wasting time, energy and money. Imagine trying to sail from one port to another without a navigational plan. You would spend your time continually trying to find direction, and simply to make port.

Without a plan to operate by you will be 'fighting fires' most of the time, and will find it difficult to maintain your focus. Good planning is like an efficiently working radar system. It keeps us on beam, and even though we may have emergencies and important issues arise which temporarily distract us, we will always come back on beam again.

- *Make time for breakfast.* It is important that you get your blood sugar level up early in the day if it is to be maintained efficiently all day long. If you want to have a higher level of concentration, energy and also to have a buoyant rather than a depressive mood, make sure that you have breakfast. Doing so will also help you to avoid that mid-afternoon slump time which is so common in industry. You wouldn't run your Rolls Royce without fuel would you? Is your body less important than this?

- *Know yourself* — you are your biggest and most important asset. Find out (through observation) when your peak energy times are and use these times wisely. For many people their peak energy flow occurs in the morning and their energy dips somewhere around mid-afternoon. They may have a secondary peak energy time in the early or mid-evening. Your mental alertness often ties in with the times when your energy is at its highest, so learn to tap into it.

As far as you are able to, plan your active tasks to coincide with your peak energy flow, and your reactive tasks to coincide with the time when your energy is lower. Your planning, creative thinking, dealing with conflicts and difficult situations, as well as jobs which demand a high level of energy and concentration all come under the heading of active tasks. Your reactive tasks may consist of activities such as returning phone calls, follow-through work, responding to less important letters.

- *Pace yourself, and teach your people to do the same.* To do so is to learn to use your energy wisely. Many people do not work wisely and efficiently and do not know how to get the best from themselves. Take a short break at the end of every two to two-and-a-half-hours' work, and a longer break (for a meal) at the end of every four hours of work. Spend ten minutes on relaxation when you first go home in the evening, before you start your evening activities. This ensures you change your work hat for your home hat, and so give yourself better quality time with your family.

  When taking your relaxation breaks during the day, remember to refresh mentally as well as physically. Do something different for a few minutes and don't think or talk work. This is the way to keep your concentration as well as your physical energy at a high level.

- *Be strict about the starting and ending times of meetings.* They can be the greatest time-waster of all. Some organisations seem to hold an overabundance of meetings when time would be better spent in getting on with the job. Meetings have their place, but you need to be very strict about the time involved and ensure that the purpose of the meeting does not become buried under a morass of verbosity.

  Appoint a strong chairperson who will make attendees stick to the point and who is assertive enough to exercise the necessary control. The good chairperson will, however, see to it that quieter members of the team speak up and have their say. Often it is the person sitting quietly, listening and observing, who has the answer, but because they are not as confident as some of the more verbose members their input can be overlooked.

  Meetings are valuable from the point of finding and maintaining clear direction, setting goals and action plans to implement them, building and uniting the team, identifying problems and finding solutions and answers to them, etc. But they need to be strictly controlled and focused. If not they can be a waste of time.

- *Teach your team to plan their work.* If they don't they will spend all their time dealing with what crops up next and what is most pressing, (which may not be their highest priority.) The danger in not planning is that people can end up being disorganised all day.

- *The first five minutes of your working day are the most important.* Arrive five minutes earlier if you have to, to give yourself time to write your priority list, or to review it if you wrote it just prior to leaving work the night before. Get things on paper, this is the way to keep your focus throughout the day and to keep ensuring that you go back to what is a real priority when you are pulled away to cope with emergencies. If you have not learnt how to organise yourself and plan your work then take a time management seminar, and get those members of your team who have not previously attended one to join you as well. Learning how to organise oneself and one's time pays off again and again. The busier you are the more you will have to organise and plan. Doing so will free you up to get on with the more important aspects of your job and to think creatively. To fail to do so is not only to waste your time, talents and skills, but also to cause yourself unnecessary stress and to risk losing direction.

If you want to be free to think creatively and deeply, and to have a clear overview of what you are doing and where you are going, you must get yourself organised. If you want your team to work with maximum efficiency as well, make sure they know how to organise themselves and their work.

3. Have your long-term goals always in focus.

- *Do not get side-tracked* with short-term goals and emergency situations. Certainly you have to deal with these, but beware the 'fighting fires' syndrome. This is why it is important to write down your long-term goals and then break them down into stepping-stone goals. You should schedule time each week (at a minimum, fortnightly) so that you can maintain direction and not get derailed by the day-to-day jobs which will always be there. It is very difficult to keep focused if you are not regularly reassessing and fine-tuning your goals and checking where you are with them. Also look at the long-term repercussions of the decisions you make. Ask yourself what these will be every time you have to make a major decision.

- *Schedule time to spend working with your people on their goals* besides continuing to set and work on your own. This will motivate them and help them to maintain impetus and direction. It will also help them to see and realise their own potential. Your job is to hold before them a vision of what they can become, and are capable of becoming in the future. Once they realise that you are aware of their potential, they will become increasingly motivated to achieve it and to give of their best.

- *Is everybody pulling in the same direction?* Does everybody have a clear understanding of their role? Often there is conflict because people are not pulling in the same direction and do not have a clear understanding of what the company or team objectives are. This happens in a surprising number of cases, and the wise leader will frequently assess the situation and find out if everyone does have the same overall goal in mind. Much confusion and disharmony can result where people's understanding of issues is hazy.

In keeping with this, the leader should discuss with individuals their particular role within the organisation. What is their job specification? What is their primary function in the company?

There is a true story told in this regard. A man who had shown promise when recruited was working very inefficiently and seemed to have the wrong focus in his job. Finally, acting on advice, his manager asked him to write his own job specification in order to clarify things for him. The manager (who incidentally had also employed him) did the same. When they compared the job specifications they were entirely different, and in fact there was only one compatible point! No wonder the poor man had not been doing well. His manager had one expectation of him and he thought he was expected to fill an entirely different role. How often, I wonder, is this situation repeated?

- *Be aware of the power of emotion.* Feelings are perhaps the most powerful motivating factor there is. Of course we have to deal in facts and in a factual way, but do not overlook the power of emotion. It is very difficult to inspire anybody to achieve a goal unless you can make them feel strongly about it. Making a scenario come alive for them so that they can see it, feel it, breathe it and taste it, is one of the best motivational tools there is. Unless you convey emotions through your words it is doubtful that you will really motivate anybody.

- *Use contracts, if necessary, to motivate people.* Some people are hard to motivate. They may need to see something on paper in the form of a contract they can strive to achieve and measure up to. They may also need the incentive of having a measuring format by which they can assess their progress and performance. A contract regarding the achievement of goals (which is broken down to a step-by-step process) may be what they need to measure their performance and progress by. If this is so, draw one up with them, and jointly assess progress through working to it.

  Sometimes, because a particular person's learning mode is mainly visual, they may need to have something in writing. So if you have people whom you seem to be unable to motivate, try getting things down on paper with them. This gives them something concrete that they can see and work to. Other people may also need written measurements in order to start and assess their progress.

  If you can teach the team how to measure and evaluate their work this adds interest and gives them a feeling of responsibility. People like to measure their performance; they get satisfaction from doing so. It's also something to strive against, e.g., trying to beat their own record for the last month. You can, if you wish, ask members of the team to evaluate each other as long as this is done in a positive way, and with everybody's consent. This can be useful. People have a great need for recognition and positive feedback.

4. Develop your people management skills.

- *Be prepared to do your best for all people,* and this includes both clients and staff. Doing so really pays off. People remember that you cared enough to put yourself out and do your best for them at the time. You know the universal and spiritual law of return. Simply put, it is 'If you want to get — give.' I once gained a very big contract for ongoing training programmes to a particularly large organisation as a result of a favour I did somebody in that organisation ten years previously. I had forgotten the favour, but they hadn't. The competition was fierce for this contract, but they spoke up for me, and as a result I was chosen to do the job (they had also followed my work and thought I could deliver the goods as well, so by speaking up for me they didn't compromise their integrity).

You never know when what you do is going to have repercussions but you can be sure that it *will* have repercussions. Whether or not they are to your advantage is up to you. If you follow the principle of showing you care, to both your staff and clients, you will build a very positive reputation for yourself, one which will stand you in good stead and grow over the years. Quite apart from the principle at stake here, you are writing yourself an insurance policy for the future by doing so.

- *Be very careful that you do not play favourites.* People will lose their trust and confidence in you in double-quick time if you indulge in this kind of game-playing; it is destructive in the extreme. We must treat everybody the same way, even though we cannot like everybody equally. You are not responsible for your feelings, but only for the way you act and your attitude towards people.

Even those on the positive, receiving end of your 'playing favourites' will ultimately lose respect for you if you try this negative and damaging game. So don't let the emotion of liking or disliking get in the way of your integrity regarding the way you treat people. Your staff deserve to know that they will be treated fairly, impartially and well by you in all circumstances.

- *We teach people how to treat us.* It is a fact of life that people will treat us as we expect to be treated. They take their cue from us. If we respect ourselves then they will also respect us. It follows that, if we have a healthy respect for ourselves, we are not going to allow other people to put us down, use us, take advantage of us or treat us with a lack of respect. People quickly learn from our attitude towards ourselves and others, and will instinctively know how far they can go with us and how much respect we expect from them — and it is difficult if not impossible to influence people unless they first respect us.

- *What are you rewarding*? When dealing with your people, ask yourself this question. Quick-fix answers? Appearance of busyness? Always doing things in an orderly and structured way? Avoiding making mistakes? Assuming total responsibility for the job (in which case there could be a failure to delegate occurring)? Sticking with the status quo and being very careful at all times? Excessive report writing? Keeping a tight rein on everyone and everything?

The above all add up to a person who is busy but not efficient, who is playing it safe but who is never being innovative, taking calculated risks, or even thinking creatively. Go out on a limb and, within reason, encourage people to take calculated risks, be innovative, extend themselves and experiment. This way you are encouraging lèarning and growth.

- *Ensure that people do not feel that they are just cogs in the wheel.* It is important that everyone knows how their particular area of responsibility contributes to the overall result, and that their individual job is important to the organisational goal. People who feel that they are valued both for themselves and for their skills are far more likely to be motivated, to show commitment to their job and to work well consistently. Also, on a practical level, people are then much less likely to sabotage the work by, for instance, grumbling or undermining of management policies, if they feel an important part of the organisation as a whole.

- *Do not overlook the quiet people* who steadily and consistently spend their time doing their very best for the organisation, sometimes in the face of considerable difficulty. These are the people who are the unsung heroes. They are always there, and can be relied on. Regardless of the pressure they may be under or what else is going on in their lives, they just quietly and consistently get on with the job and 'deliver the goods'. Only too often these people are unappreciated and overlooked. They should be rewarded for their loyalty and commitment. Make sure that you frequently affirm and acknowledge these valuable people — they deserve it!

- *Don't condemn out of hand those team members who do not appear to be doing well.* Before you think too badly of them, or even demote them, ask yourself what the problem is. In many instances a large part of the fault lies with management. The person concerned may not have been given proper training to do their job efficiently. Sometimes they are working in impossibly difficult circumstances. Very often people do not fully understand what is expected of them, because nobody takes the time and trouble to explain this to them. Then again, they may not have received the specific help they need to overcome their areas of inadequacy, for instance being sent on an organisational and time management seminar if they have proved unable to organise their work well and manage their time efficiently. Quite often a heart-to-heart talk in a supportive atmosphere with their manager or team leader will bring factors to light which were previously unknown, and then the problem may well resolve itself.

In one instance I was asked to work with the manager of a department store, who was handling her staff very badly. It turned out that this lady had very low self-esteem and was terribly lacking in confidence. After giving her a confidence building course, and also arranging for someone to support her when she felt she needed it, she improved to a marked degree. In fact she positively blossomed, and in the end became one of the best and most popular managers this chain of stores had. So before you jump to a negative conclusion, look for the broader (and perhaps less obvious) answers.

• *Do your best for your customers.* You are dependent upon your customers for your existence; they have priority, and they deserve the best in every sense. Sometimes organisations get so involved in process, structuring and the technicalities of what they do and how they do it, that they lose sight of the most important thing of all — their customers. It pays to remind people regularly that the customer is *essential* to your remaining in business and to everybody retaining their job.

People talk. If you have satisfied customers who have learnt to trust you and the quality of your service and goods, you have the best advertisement of the lot. Whether your customers are well treated or badly treated they *will talk*, and they are more likely to talk if they are dissatisfied. When you get to the stage where you are getting call-back business or are gaining new customers through word of mouth recommendation, you will know you have made it. Satisfied customers are your best source of generating business.

5. Strive constantly for quality of performance.

• *Quality brings lasting results,* while lack of quality may bring a quick result but will never give a lasting one. Quality involves a commitment to doing things right and in the best possible way every time. It also involves measuring standards of efficiency and performance, taking time to think things through and not just going for the quick-fix answer.

A good way to check quality is to ask the person responsible for their ideas on how their aspect of the work can be improved. Nobody knows their job better than the person who does it day in day out. The wise manager recognises this and utilises this tremendous source they have available to them. Also, be quick to reward enthusiasm and commitment to improving standards. This is a very good way to keep steadily checking and improving quality. It is also a great motivator. Insofar as is possible, allow people to work in the way that is right for them. If they can do it their way they will feel greater commitment to doing the job as well as they possibly can. Again, the wise leader or manager caters for individual needs and allows an opportunity for an expression of people's creativity. The long-term payoffs for doing so are incalculable. So don't make the mistake of overstructuring. Just because a thing has always been done in a certain way doesn't mean that there are advantages in continuing to do it that way.

As long as you get quality in results you want to give as much freedom and flexibility as possible in the *way* things are done. Don't take the incentive for being creative and innovative from your personnel. Make them feel like winners and let them know you see them as winners. Remember, being fully involved and having a say in how things are done produces good results, which in turn helps people to feel good about themselves. This must lead to greater commitment to quality performance.

- *Don't just accept the status quo* and encourage your people not to either. Spend time thinking things through. There is always a better way, and through thinking creatively and experimenting, you and your people will find it.

- *Don't ever worry about people making mistakes.* Worry if they're not. This indicates that, for some reason, they are afraid to think creatively, extend, be innovative and try new ways. Encourage and reward people for trying to find better ways of doing things, even if it does involve a few mistakes. Intelligent mistake-making is the price we pay for progress. Eventually people either learn from their mistakes (and therefore make what they were trying to achieve work) or they find better ways of doing it. Making mistakes is a sign of people on the move. Never worry when you see it happening.

6. Value your team.

- *Get to know your team's areas of strength and weakness.* Build on their strengths and in a positive, non-judgemental and caring way help them to overcome their areas of weakness. Remember, too, that by admitting yours you will make it safe for them to admit theirs.

- *Discover the rewards people want,* remembering that these rewards may not always involve money. Different individuals have different needs, and are satisfied by different things. The wise leader finds out what gives individual members of the team the most satisfaction and fulfilment in the form of rewards, and what is most significant to them. For one it is time off, for another it is public recognition, for another it is receiving an additional official title, for another it is being allowed to choose the job that they enjoy doing the most, for another it is being given the opportunity of running a group session or doing a case study for the group, for another it may be something more tangible — for example, a new piece of equipment. Rewards do not all have to be the same. Cater to people's individuality and learn what 'turns them on'.

- *Give frequent feedback to both individuals and to the team.* No feedback is in fact a sign of rejection. I often quote the true story of the man who worked for the same firm for 38 years. Upon his retirement he was amazed to hear the number of positive statements made about him by his superiors. After his retirement function had ended he commented to one of his colleagues, 'It was very gratifying to hear all those positive things my employers said about me, but how I wish I had heard some of them during the 38 years I have been working for them. It would have meant so much to me then, and probably would have inspired me to better performance.' Only too often in industry the 'no news is good news' syndrome is the rule. People need regular and positive feedback; one of our basic needs as human beings is to know how we are doing.

- *A good leader almost works themselves out of a job.* You should train your people up to the point where they can take over and lead, as well as keep the show afloat if you happen to be off work for any reason. Training people up to this point of competency is a long-term investment. It is important that your people know that you have faith in them and that you trust them to handle things well, to be innovative, come up with creative solutions and to make wise decisions. (Conversely, they should learn when to stop short of making decisions which they recognise they are not at this time capable of making.) In other words, encourage them to extend, but also to know their limitations.

  There are enormous pay-offs in investing in people in this way. As they become increasingly competent and their confidence grows, they also become increasingly valuable to both the team leader and the organisation as a whole. The interest on your personal investment of time and energy in your people will be incalculable in the future.

- *Accelerated learning.* One of the most exciting tools to come to the fore recently is that of accelerated learning. This is based on the premise that our brain operates in different ways according to our individuality, and that we all have different modes of learning. We receive, process, understand and use information in different ways. The leader who wishes to help his or her people to function best will learn all they can about these techniques, and will arrange for their staff members to do the same.

- *Get personal support.* Regardless of how strong you think you are, or how well you think you are handling things, you will always go better if you have personal support. Therefore build your own support systems around you, and use them frequently. Sharing and having other like-minded, positively thinking people involved will undoubtedly enable you to function better; it will also act as a catalyst to your own creative thinking. It's lonely at the top, and the higher you go the lonelier it gets, so don't make the mistake of trying to 'go it alone' — it's the quickest way to burn out or crash. Encourage your team to use support systems, too. The team as a whole will certainly function better and ultimately deliver better results.

7. Work at your decision-making and problem-solving skills.

- *Try not to make major decisions when you are feeling under stress.* This is the time when you are likely to make mistakes because your perspective alters, and you lose your ability to see the picture as a whole. A characteristic of the stressed person is that they can only see what is happening immediately under their nose, or one segment of the whole, but do not have the ability to see the long-term and total overview of the situation. If people are pressuring you for a decision (and it is an important issue) tell them you need more time to think it through. You can say something like 'Do you want a quick decision, or would you rather wait for the right one?' If in doubt always ask for time, write out as much as you can, including the pros and cons regarding the problem, get the best advice you can (even if you have to pay for it) and sleep on it. If you are really being pressured and are still not sure, the situation may allow you to make an interim decision. However, also make it clear that this is not the final decision, and that it will be reviewed and possibly changed within a short time. If it is not possible to take this latter course of action, then hold out for time until you are sure. Consult with people whose judgement you trust then go for what feels right and gives you the most peace of mind.

- *The buck stops here.* Though you are wise to ask many opinions and to seek the best advice you can, there will be times when you must be the one to make the final decision. Certainly weigh up and consider everything everybody tells you, but at the end of the day you stand or fall by the decision you make so, provided it is within your area of expertise and responsibility, you should be the one to make it.

Sometimes people can be very persuasive in the advice they give you, but it pays to remember that other people can only come from the basis of their own experience and knowledge, and this may be no better than yours. If they have had more experience than you regarding the particular situation, or if they are professionals in their field, then of course you will pay more attention to the advice they give. Beyond this, however, remember that what other people tell you is based on their experience and is often no better than an opinion.

- *When faced with people problems and difficult situations confront, don't ignore.* One of the biggest mistakes the leader or manager can make is to shut their eyes and hope that it will all go away. You can bet your bottom dollar it won't. Problems involving people do not usually just fade away and disappear, rather they tend to steadily build up. So deal with the problem when it is smaller rather than bigger; that way it can quickly be sorted out.

- *Prepare people for the tough jobs.* Warn them that the job is going to be tough, and what they can expect, but do so in a positive way. Talk about it in terms of it being a challenge, and also along the lines of 'If we can do this we can handle anything they can throw at us.' Let them know that you have faith in them and their ability to handle it. Also that you are going to be there in an active (if possible) and/or supportive role. Involve them in this prior discussion, and ask them for ideas as to how this job can be made easier or can be made to run more smoothly. Ask for their help. People will take their attitude from you, and if you are straight with them about the difficulties of the job, but also have a positive attitude towards it they will be prepared in a positive way. Try also to show your faith and confidence in their ability to handle it, and you will psychologically prepare them to do so. Emphasise the challenge aspect of the job.

- *Learn to compartmentalise.* This is one of the most valuable skills known to people who are busy and people who carry responsibility. It involves being able to see a project or problem as a whole, but breaking it down into workable compartments (bite-size pieces). Sometimes, when we look at a project or job in its entirety, it may seem to be too much. However if we can divide it into manageable sections and focus on completing one section at a time, the whole thing becomes workable and manageable. Compartmentalising involves cultivating the mental skill of being able to switch off to the project as a whole and focus only on the part we are working on at the time.

The principle, however, goes deeper than that. It also includes learning the mental discipline of switching off to that which is completed, and that which is yet to come, and focusing only on the work we are actually doing at the time.

This requires much practice, but the advantages are enormous. For one thing it greatly reduces our stress levels. For another, it enables us to concentrate better on the work in hand. Another advantage is that we learn to conserve energy and direct it only to that which we are working on at the time, a skill that is almost essential to the person who is very busy or carrying heavy responsibilities.

The reality is that we are only actually existing *in this moment* in which we are alive. Five minutes ago is history, and we don't even know that we have five minutes hence. Therefore *we only have to meet the demands of the moment.* When you adopt this principle you will be able compartmentalise more effectively. You have only to meet the demands of the moment in which you are now living, breathing, working. A practical application of this principle is first of all to organise your work in order of priority, then put all work except that which you have to do at this moment to one side. Concentrate totally on the job which you are now doing, and when it is completed, cross it off your list and move it somewhere else, mentally switching off from it. Now, give your total concentration and attention to the job with the next highest priority. Always make sure that you have only one job on your desk at a time of course. You will find this a very good habit which will stand you in good stead all through life, and prevent much stress.

If I had not learnt to compartmentalise some years ago, I could not do all the things I now have to do in the course of my day, which may involve counselling somebody, preparing a talk, writing a chapter of my current book, making managerial decisions to do with the running of my organisation, giving a half-day training session to some corporation, dealing with a myriad of phone calls, interacting with my husband and family. It is through this skill that I am able to keep switching hats and cope! I think it is one of the most useful tools I have ever added to my toolkit.

- *Take action, don't get anxious.* This is a maxim I would recommend to you. Once more it is a great stress-breaker and will save anxiety building up to the point where you become really stressed. Always deal with your problems in a practical way. To do nothing is to invite worry. When we fail to take any action regarding our problems we divert our energy to become internal anxiety. Taking action — even as small as picking up the phone and asking for more information — directs energy outwardly in a positive way. So always *do something.* Write a list of pros and cons or advantages and disadvantages, talk the problem over with someone whose judgement you trust, seek more information, take that first small decisive step towards solving the problem. It doesn't matter in which order you do these things, but do *something.*

Problem-solving is a step-by-step process. There is a saying, 'God can't steer a car that's stalled but He can steer one that is in motion.' How true. When you take that first small step you are setting in motion a process which will ultimately lead to the resolving of your problem, and there is far greater chance that the next step will also become apparent. It's great to have such clear direction that the outcome is very clear to you. This is what we would all like to happen. Unfortunately life isn't always like that. Often it is not until we are actually moving one step at a time towards solving a problem, that we can actually see the end result. What will inhibit you and rob you of your energy and clear focus in solving problems is anxiety.

- *Don't add unnecessary stress through inaction.* There is quite enough stress in most jobs these days without allowing more to accumulate by failing to address underlying issues, unresolved problems, negative relationships, old-fashioned, cumbersome work methods, insufficient information or resources . . . we could go on and on. Confront the issues; if you don't they will add to your stress level and will rob you of energy and concentration. Make a list of those things which need to be dealt with and are holding you and the organisation back from functioning efficiently and well. Define a time-plan in which to deal with them. Don't put up with emotionally draining, undermining, negative factors which rob you of your peace of mind and make your job more difficult.

- *Simple answers are usually the best,* and the most profound. In all disciplines people will tell you that the simpler the answer the better it usually is. Be suspicious of anything complicated. Some people delight in creating 'wheels within wheels', taking a simple issue and making it obscure and difficult. The most brilliant answers are usually very simple in essence.

- *Access to information.* Nowadays it is impossible to carry the amount of information you need in your head. It is not important that you know everything about your job, but it is important that you know where to go to quickly find out the information you need to do your job well. Make it your business to find out where you can quickly and readily access information, and make sure your people know how to do this too.

- *Finally, look to a higher power than yourself for help.* This is a very personal point, and you may choose to ignore it if you do not believe in God.

Personally I do, and I believe that God is the source of all power, true guidance and love. I have received enormous help in acknowledging that I do not know all the answers, and often do not have the wisdom or strength to do all that I am called upon to do, but that I have a higher power (God) who dwells within, and who is there to release in me what I need in order to function well.

I believe that I have only to tap into God's strength and I will receive the strength to do what I have to well, and also receive the guidance and direction I need. Which is not to say that I do not have to use every ounce of my own commonsense, logic, and ability to analyse and think things through, in order to arrive at the right conclusion.

Relying on God to 'fuel the fire' is not in any way to absolve us from doing our best to handle the situations and problems we are called upon to deal with. It does mean acknowledging and being open to the influence of a greater power than ourselves, while at the same time extending ourselves as fully as possible to realise our God-given potential. I believe that both are compatible and both are necessary.

So don't stress yourself too much and become bowed down under the weight of your responsibility and demands, but rather turn inwardly to the source of all power and knowledge, who is there for you in the fullest sense of the expression. The busier you are, the more you need to take a few quiet minutes daily to pray and meditate, opening your consciousness to God — because therein lies your strength, wisdom and guidance.

APPENDIX

Two company communication models

As I have frequently stated throughout this book, nothing improves until people begin communicating. A company communication model is a good starting point to get good communication flowing. Use the following sample models, one for a smaller and one for a larger organisation, to draw up your own company communication model – one which is right for your company's particular needs.

SMALL ORGANISATION

DAILY

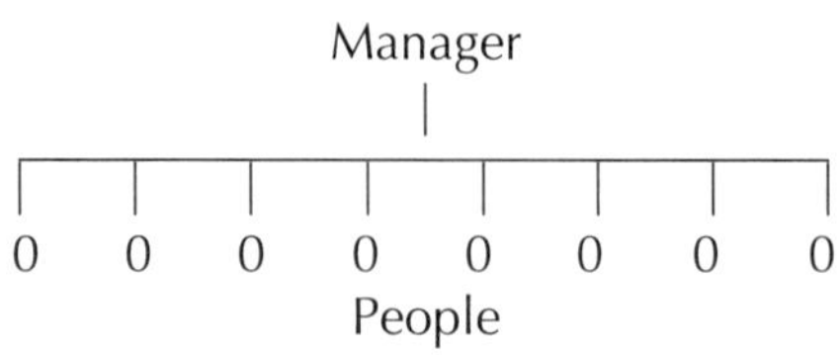

- Manager spends five minutes daily with each member of the team.

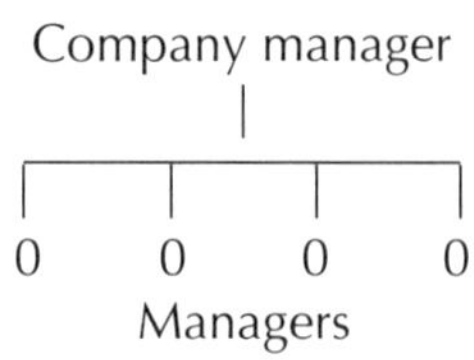

- Company manager and managers meet for twenty minutes daily after morning tea when managers have had time to visit team and assess working situation.

WEEKLY

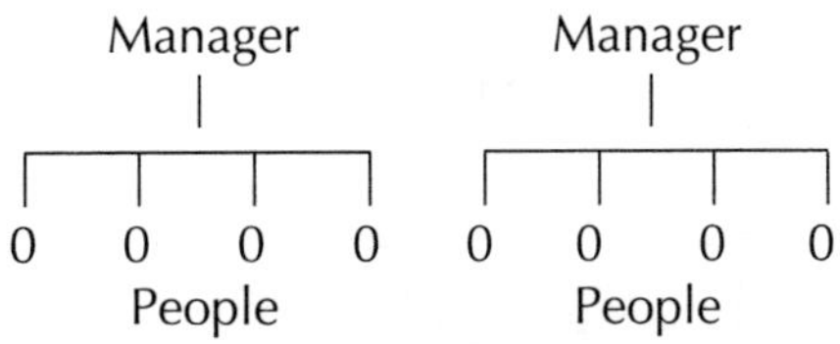

- Manager splits people into two teams (maximum of four people per team) for a one hour meeting each week.

- Structure of meeting:

First 15 minutes:	identifying problems.
Second 15 minutes:	brainstorming for solutions; exploring options.
Third 15 minutes:	affirming.
Fourth 15 minutes:	discussing change (real and hoped for).

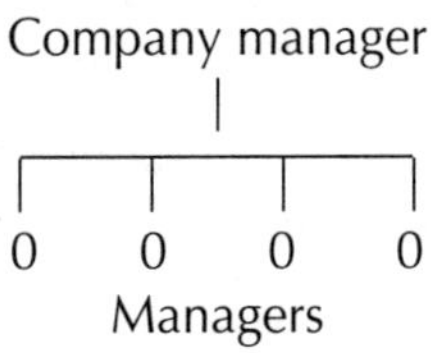

- Full meeting of company manager and managers to discuss results of above, plus other business. Meeting time: $1\frac{1}{2}$ hours.

- Friday night: Happy hour, all staff.

(All models shown on pages 200 – 205 © Iris Barrow)

MONTHLY

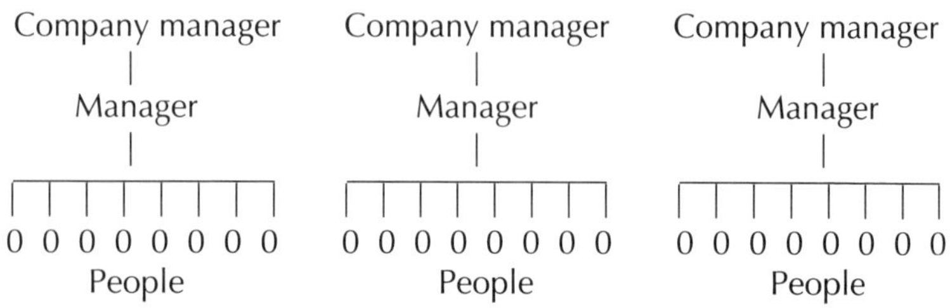

- Company manager and manager sit in on monthly manager/team meetings , listening, clarifying, forecasting direction.

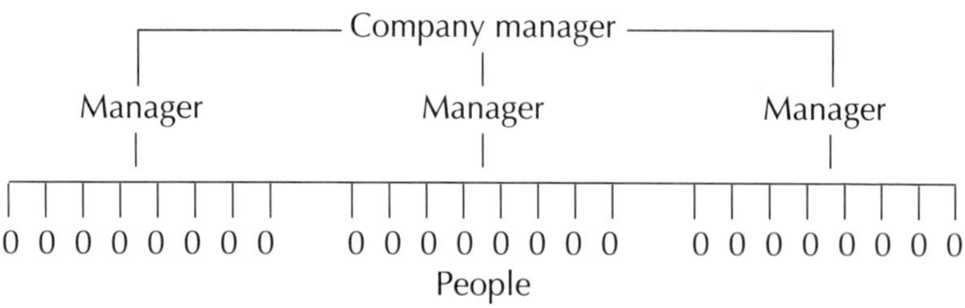

- *Ritual:* Social get-together of all staff and families: e.g. barbeque, ten-pin bowling, cricket match, picnic, etc.

LARGER ORGANISATION

DAILY

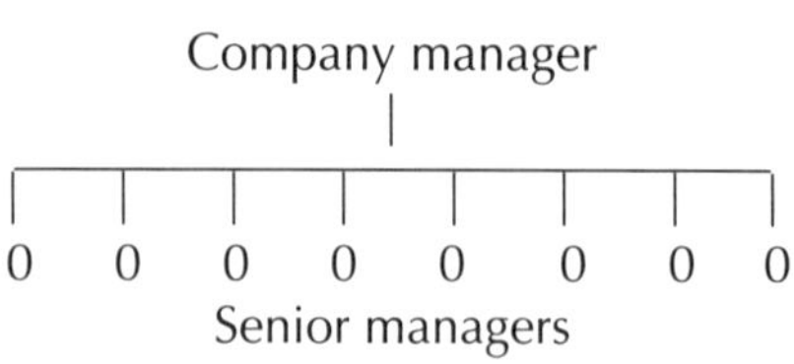

- Company manager and senior managers meet for half an hour at the same time daily.

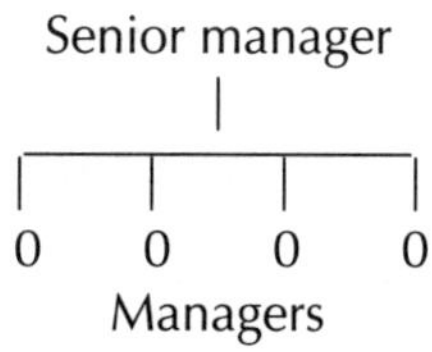

- Senior manager meets with managers for twenty minutes daily at the same time: e.g., after morning tea.

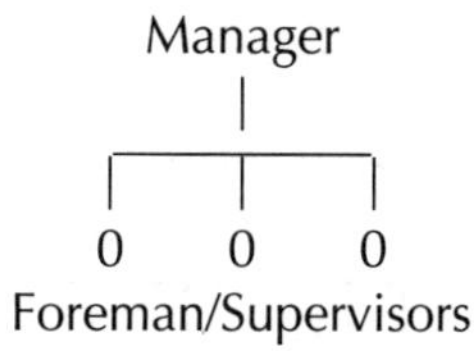

- Manager meets with foreman/supervisors for twenty minutes daily at the same time: e.g., after the above meeting.

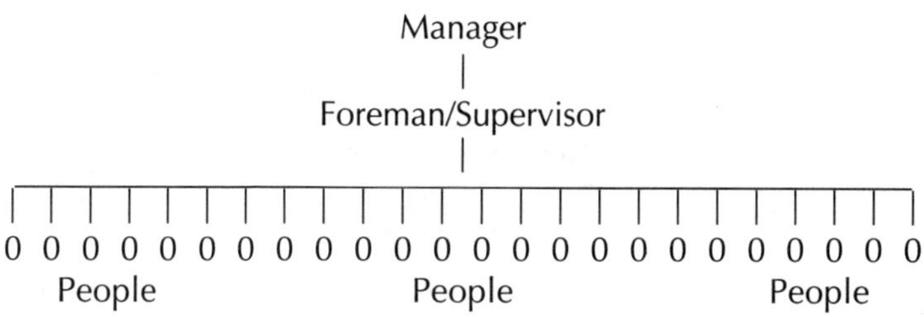

- Manager spends two minutes daily communicating with as many personnel as possible.

- Foreman/supervisors spend five minutes daily communicating with each team member.

WEEKLY

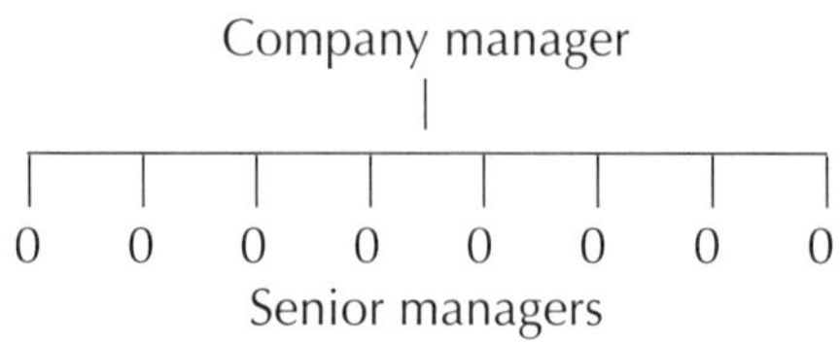

- Full meeting of all senior managers and company manager to discuss results of what has flowed up through pipeline (below); plus other business. Meeting time: 1½ hours.

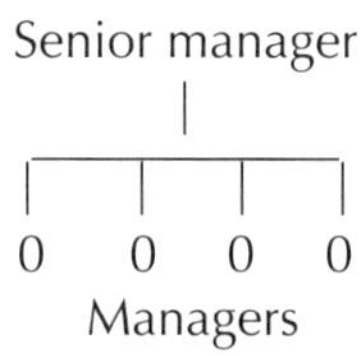

- Full meeting of all senior managers and managers to discuss results of what has flowed up through pipeline and structure (below); plus general business. Meeting time: 1½ hours.

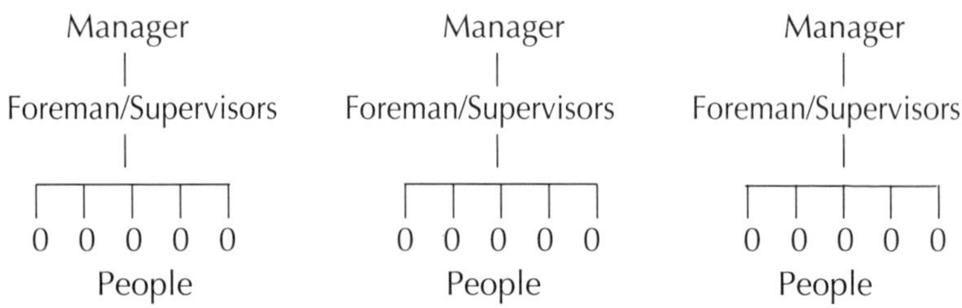

- Meeting of foreman/supervisors and all personnel (six personnel per meeting). Manager to attend as time permits.

- Structure of each one hour meeting:
  First 15 minutes: identifying problems.
  Second 15 minutes: brainstorming for solutions; exploring options.
  Third 15 minutes: affirming.
  Fourth 15 minutes: discussing change (real and hoped for).

MONTHLY

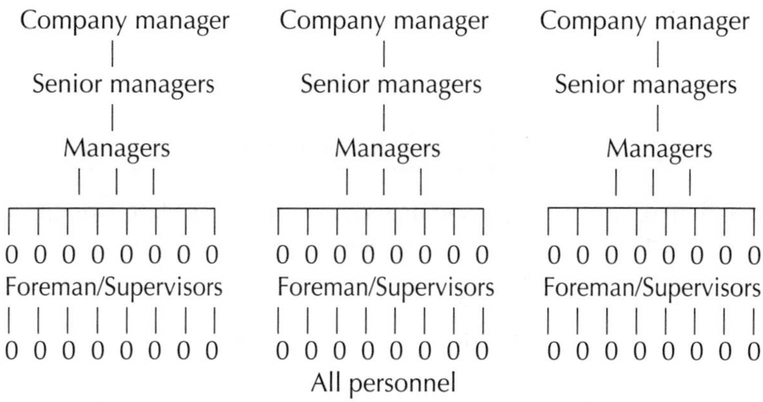

- Senior managers, managers, foremen, supervisors and all personnel have monthly team meetings. Company manager and observer attend one or two meetings a month. Purpose of meeting: listening, clarifying, forecasting direction.

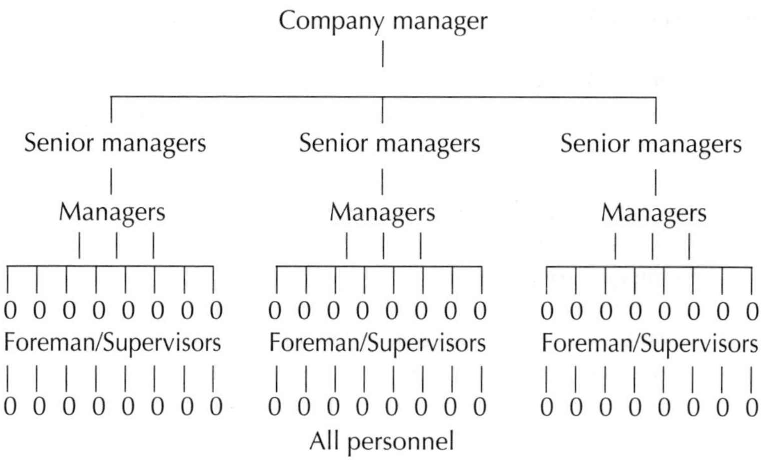

- *Ritual:* Social get-together of all staff and families; e.g. barbeque, ten-pin bowling, cricket match, picnic, show (block booking), trip (one day), etc.

SEMINARS AND SELF-HELP TAPES

Iris Barrow presents personal and interpersonal skills seminars internationally. For details, please send for her business brochure to:

Iris Barrow
13 Hostel Access Rd
Eastern Beach
Auckland
New Zealand
Phone (09) 534-2697

There are eight learning tapes available for people who wish to acquire further skills. These reinforce the message of Iris Barrow's books. They are:

1 **Learning to Relax**. Five ten-minute mental and physical relaxation exercises. Where two exercises are listened to daily, improvement usually takes place within three weeks.

2 **Understanding and Overcoming Stress**. All about understanding, identifying and learning how to cope with stress. Practical ways of overcoming and controlling it.

3 **Understanding and Overcoming Depression**. A series of simple steps to help overcome depression and prevent its recurrence. Better ways of functioning outlined.

4 **Raising Your Self-esteem**. Methods for raising self-esteem (includes exercises). Having good self-esteem is vital to mental and emotional wellbeing. We can only act 'out there' according to how we feel within ourselves.

5 **How to Build Your Confidence**. Ways of building confidence, based on acting as we wish to become, and feeding in positive messages to achieve results and help us grow on all levels.

6 **Responsible Self-assertion**. Ways of being assertive without harming others' rights and feelings. How to handle anger and criticism and express these emotions, say no constructively, set limits and be compassionate, while avoiding being manipulative.

7 **Communicate with Confidence**. Keys to communicating in a relaxed and confident way, overcoming shyness, listening skills, drawing people out, speaking up in a group, how to communicate effectively and reach people.

8 **Goal Setting and Motivation**. How to set and achieve your goals; includes how to motivate yourself to achieve your potential and become successful and fulfilled.

Also available is a half-hour video, **Celebrating Life With Iris Barrow**, in which Iris presents life skills for better functioning.

Audio tapes last sixty minutes. Overall price, including a set of instructions where appropriate (prices valid at time of going to press):

One tape	$16.00	Five tapes	$64.50
Two tapes	$30.00	Six tapes	$76.00
Three tapes	$41.50	Seven tapes	$87.50
Four tapes	$53.00	Eight tapes	$99.00

Video tape	$38.50

N.B. Discount applies to any combination of tapes. Postage and packaging within New Zealand is included in price. Please post the order form overleaf to Mrs Iris Barrow at the address given.

ORDER FORM

Complete and return to:

Iris Barrow
13 Hostel Access Rd
Eastern Beach
Auckland
New Zealand

Please send me (tick)

1 ( ) Learning to Relax
2 ( ) Understanding and Overcoming Stress
3 ( ) Understanding and Overcoming Depression
4 ( ) Raising Your Self-esteem
5 ( ) How to Build Your Confidence
6 ( ) Responsible Self-assertion
7 ( ) Communicate with Confidence
8 ( ) Goal Setting and Motivation

Video tape ( ) Celebrating Life with Iris Barrow

I enclose a cheque for $...........

Please post tapes to:

NAME..
ADDRESS..
....

These tapes are also available in Australia. For information/brochure please write to:

Iris Barrow Tapes
Mr Frank E. Newstead — Success Centre
P.O. Box 333
Balwyn 3103
Australia
Phone (03) 830-1944